D1453211

Border-Crossing Spirituality

Border-Crossing Spirituality

Transformation in the Borderland

JUNG EUN SOPHIA PARK, SNJM

PICKWICK *Publications* • Eugene, Oregon

BORDER-CROSSING SPIRITUALITY
Transformation in the Borderland

Pickwick Publications
An Imprint of Wipf and Stock Publishers
199 W. 8th Ave., Suite 3
Eugene, OR 97401

www.wipfandstock.com

PAPERBACK ISBN: 978-1-4982-2600-4
HARDCOVER ISBN: 978-1-4982-2602-8
ELECTRONIC ISBN: 978-1-4982-2601-1

Cataloguing-in-Publication data:

Name: Park, Jung Eun Sophia, SNJM.
Title: Border-crossing spirituality : transformation in the borderland / Jung Eun Sophia Park, SNJM.
Description: Eugene, OR : Pickwick, 2016 | Includes bibliographical references.
Identifiers: ISBN 978-1-4982-2600-4 (paperback) | ISBN 978-1-4982-2602-8 (hardcover) | ISBN 978-1-4982-2601-1 (ebook)
Subjects: LCSH: Cultural pluralism. | Group identity. | Spirituality. | Emigration and immigration. | Liminality—Religious aspects.
Classification: LCC JV6091 P15 2016 (print) | LCC JV6091 (ebook)

Manufactured in the U.S.A. 06/20/16

Contents

Introduction

In our global and multicultural society, many people experience border crossings, which include several layered significations in terms of geography, culture, economy, and spirituality. Border-crossing is a polyvalent and multilayered reality. On the geographical level, border crossings occur today due to mass migration, resulting in many people living in an experience of dislocation. While some people must cross borders for survival, fleeing violence and war, other people from the third world cross borders in search of a better life, often risking their lives. This phenomenon creates a new cultural map around the world, creating a kind of third culture.

Also, border crossings occur due to the tsunami of information obtained through social media. Much knowledge and endless ideas are shared quickly by encountering different cultures and religions. Popular culture, such as K-pop from South Korea, is famous in the United States and many other countries. A prominent theorist of political sciences, the scholar Samuel Huntington, predicted that the world would be reconstructed according to cultures and, more specifically, to religions, and even warned that we would live in the terror and violence caused by the so-called "war" of religions.[1] This has somewhat come to fruition: we hear about many tragedies due to an intolerance of religions. Despite this prominent notion of Huntington, "the war" of religions, we also

1. See Huntington, *Clash of Civilizations*.

see a different picture in our time, which emphasizes interreligious and cross-cultural dynamics.

Many immigrants and their following generations, called hybrid people, are shaping the third culture. For example, in Oakland, California, one of the most diverse societies in the United States, many college students prefer to claim themselves as Californians rather than identifying with any specific label of religion, ethnicity, or race. The reason is that they are living in an interracial and intercultural way. For them, it is almost impossible to address themselves with singular labels, such as "Asian" or "Hispanic." They respect the complexity of their lineage by saying, for instance, "I am a quarter Asian, quarter Hispanic, quarter Native American, and quarter Irish." Similarly, people often say, "I do not have a religious affiliation, but I engage in various spiritual practices." They are called *NRBS*—not religious, but spiritual—or *NONE*, which implies that they do not have any specific religious affiliation. Today, many people claim multiple religious belongings.[2] Many people live in an interreligious or intercultural way, and this way of being indicates a border-crossing lifestyle.

In looking at border-crossings in terms of the whole human experience, the existential aspect of border crossings should be considered, too. Observing human life, it is obvious that every person's life is composed of transitions of sorts and of border-crossings. We are tempted to understand life as a linear continuum, but it is rather arbitrary. As a matter of fact, life is always transient and life itself is a process. From infancy to childhood, or from youth to young adulthood, or from middle age to old age, life flows as a process and every moment is composed of border crossings.

Often, during obvious transitional periods, such as marriage, divorce, and retirement, people experience great turmoil and vulnerability. In actuality, everybody lives within the process and every moment exists as an *in-between* moment: between the past and the future. Therefore, we can say that we live a life of border-crossing and stay in the borderland. In the mythology of various cultures, death, in relation to life, is understood as a border-crossing; we live

2. Cornille, "Multiple Religious Belonging," 329.

in a liminal space between death and life. The border-crossing nature of life constitutes the ontological condition of human beings. This teaching has been repeated in various religions.

Significantly, relationship or dialogue with other human beings, nature, and with God is an important aspect of life, and a gateway to knowledge[3]; an authentic relationship necessarily includes border-crossing. Through relationships, an individual person crosses over one's own boundaries and enters into a new dimension of life. The relationship indicates a border-crossing, through which an individual will be transformed. As Martin Buber asserts, when the perfect encounter is about to occur, [the gates] are unified into the one gate of actual life, and then life will be transformed.[4] Very often, the person's boundary or border is shaped by cultural, religious, or family values, and when the person is engaged with others, the person crosses borders. In the borderland space the person will experience transformation.

Recently, the notion of borderland and/or border-crossing has become popular. It has been applied to many areas of research, such as cultural studies, ethnic studies, sociology, and environmental studies, focusing on liminal status as an opportunity to gain access to new possibilities in terms of resistance, creativity, and transformation. The liminal space of the borderland is highly dangerous and violent, but active and creative as well. The creativity is apparent in constructing or deconstructing the language which functions as the fundamental frame through which the culture is constructed.

In postcolonial literature, which is deeply related to the borderland, attention is given to the language, which often is twisted or mangled. In boldness, the grammar is destroyed; and in creativeness, a new meaning is constructed. In this language, laughter and humor cracks the structure, and in so doing, a new critical meaning is created. In the borderland of US-Mexico, for example, English is enmeshed with Spanish, or vice versa. In this space, change and subversion of the oppressive social norm occurs and

3. Berling, *Understanding Other Religious Worlds*, x.

4. Buber, *I and Thou*, 150.

a new alternative culture emerges. The borderland can function as the space of empowerment and liberation for the marginalized.

A prominent postcolonial theorist, Homi Bhahba, also emphasizes the power of the manipulation of language. For Bhabha, this borderland or third space is a constructed space at the inner city café of the metropolitan city. In this book, I heavely rely on the concept of the third space which comes from Homi Bhabha. In the café, the experience of exile or immigration is exchanged and, through the encounter, a new discourse and even new languages are created. Similarly, the late Korean American Cha Hak Kyoung, in her book *Dictée*, expresses the power of language and the powerlessness of losing her native language, and creates a borderland space where she is poised in terms of the struggles of immigrant life.[5] She addresses and articulates the experience of exile or immigration, and reveals the power difference between residents and new immigrants, which originates from western imperialism.

From a socio-political perspective, we can say that the borderland has functioned as a force of resistance over hegemonic or oppressive powers. Late twentieth and early twenty-first century historiography on the borderlands is the product of the dialogue among history, anthropology, ethno-history, post-colonial theory, geography, and most recently, the Atlantic framework. The works that deployed such interdisciplinary approaches have triggered new debates on the formation of and historical processes in borderland regions.[6] These include, for instance, the importance of social networks; the manipulation of imperial laws and policies by the western imperial power or capitalism and the response of indigenous groups; and the significance of ethnic and racial identities. Creative reactions to colonial powers are practiced in the borderland.

The idea of border-crossing includes not only the action of crossing borders between two countries and/or cultures, but also any actions or orientations toward crossing over from one's own comfort zone or boundary into an unknown space or otherness.

5. Kim, "Poised on the In-between," 18.

6. Prado, "Fringes of Empire," 318.

Then, border-crossing entails a deep spiritual dimension, emphasizing the process and resulting in transformation. The borderland signifies the situation where people face the process and the consequences of the action of border-crossing. The term *borderland*, which comes from the well-known Mexican-American feminist Gloria Anzaldúa, indicates a space that is in-between and a process for transformation. As a Mexican-American woman, Anzaldúa describes her marginalized—yet powerful—life journey in her seminal book, *Borderlands la Frontera: New Mestiza*. For her, the borderland is a space that she builds for herself, choosing all given cultures. In this spirit of freedom, the borderland becomes the ground she stands on, and in the space of the borderland she creates the new culture *una cultura mestiza*.[7]

Historically, the border-crossing phenomenon is not new. In the Tang dynasty of China, people crossed borders on the Silk Road. In the eleventh century, the Crusades crossed borders and as a result, Islamic cultures and Christian cultures were exchanged and philosophical and scientific knowledge was transmitted to Western Europe. As a consequence, some areas such as Spain constructed a borderland where the style of architecture and literature shows a third way.

However, as many people articulate and express in literature and art, border-crossing is not an easy process, but rather a tumultuous and dangerous one. Therefore, we cannot assume that the border-crossing action naturally provides transformation. In general, people who reside in a borderland feel trapped in-between and, as such, experience a deep sense of alienation—feeling invisible, voiceless, and powerless. A borderland is an open space with a challenge to transcend life into transformation. Then, there is a need to explore ways of surviving and, furthermore, thriving in this process. As long as we experience the phenomena of border crossing, and dwell in the borderland, we need to explore the spirituality of border-crossing and articulate how we can experience transformation.

7. Anzaldúa, *Borderlands*, 44.

Focusing on the lived experience, border-crossing spirituality emphasizes the notion of being "in-between" as a benchmark where people find wisdom, empowerment, and transformation. In spiritual growth, crossing borders—in terms of nation, gender, class, race, and economic status—is essential in deepening the knowledge of self, of others, and God or life itself. Therefore, it is not surprising that almost all spiritual teachings include the importance of border-crossings and of being in-between, as crucial experiences for transformation.

Thus, the border-crossing spirituality this book explores, by nature, is cross-cultural, includes various religious traditions, and utilizes interdisciplinary approaches, like other borderland studies. However, in using the term spirituality, border-crossing spirituality pays attention to the human experiences in personal, social, and environmental arenas, and seeks possibility for any transformation or merits in the borderland, such as gaining voice or claiming one's identity.

The border-crossing spirituality I suggest is an example of an inter-spirituality, which gathers wisdom from various areas by employing various texts from religions. Methodologically, border-crossing spirituality is interdisciplinary, utilizing various approaches of disciplines, such as biblical studies, religious studies, anthropology, and ritual studies. Furthermore, this border-crossing spirituality also explores interpersonal dynamics by examining the spiritual direction relationship, which exists in almost every religious tradition. A case study of Jeju Island, as a socio-political, environmental, and regional borderland with a strong tradition of Korean shamanic rituals, is provided. Jeju island and the shamanic rituals demonstrates strong possibility for empowerment and transformation who have experienced turmoil and trauma.

Border-crossing spirituality, which explores the significance of *being in-between*, can be delineated as staying in the present, regaining identity or sense of agency, listening to the other, and suggesting radical hospitality. These themes of spirituality, which emerge from each chapter, often intersect with other chapters and reinforce one another, although the context and historical background of each chapter is quite different. Also, the border-crossing spirituality introduced in this book is interstitial so that immigrants and non-immigrants could explore the spirituality of border crossing. While one chapter directly addresses immigrant experiences and spirituality of the immigrants, other chapters describe the human experience of alienation and exclusion as individual as well as group and, in so doing, insinuates spirituality for immigrants. Because the process-oriented nature of borderland, border-crossing action itself could be counted as borderland, and the vice versa. Thus the demarcating between the borderland and border-crossing action or movement can be blurred and the two terms could be often interchangeable.

The first chapter comes from the teachings of the Gospel as a Christian text. In Mark's Gospel, in the chosen pericope in particular, Jesus is a border-crossing person. In the narrative unit of Mark 5:21–43, Jesus moves into Gentile territory then back into a Jewish one. Here, readers encounter a woman suffering from a hemorrhage who encounters Jesus in the space of in-between.

In the chosen passage, as an ordinary dweller of liminal space or borderland, as with other female characters, the woman does not have a name. However, she is worse off than others in that she does not have anyone with her in the scene. She is alienated, powerless, and voiceless. Acting as an agent of her own life, she grasps the garment of Jesus and, as a consequence, she experiences healing. In this case, healing is not just about being healthy or free from ailments, but also about regaining social membership. This passage is unique in that the beneficiary of the healing takes the initiative, not the healer. In this borderland, the subject and the object are reversed and, in the process, the marginality of the woman is located at the center. Through the process of subversion, the woman determines to move her life forward and recovers her wholeness.

Chapter 2 is about a socio-political borderland that resists western imperial and military powers and advocates for environmental justice, in conjunction with Jeju's shamanism. This chapter shows how shamans create borderland in the ritual of *Kut*.

Fundamentally, a ritual space is a borderland, an "in-between" space between the secular world and the sacred world, and it is a liminal space for transformation. In this ritual borderland, the gods/spirits and human beings cross their respective borders to encounter and communicate.

Through the fieldwork conducted in 2011–2014 on Jeju Island, located between the Korean peninsula and Japan, I observed that border-crossing spirituality is manifested in shamanic rituals. A shaman is a guide to accompany the dead and in the borderland, which is called *Miaji Bangdi,* the soul is cleansed and experiences freedom. Literally, the term *Miaji Bangdi* means the empty space where the soul wanders, after which, when the soul is ready, it enters into the other world.

This chapter demonstrates, through an analysis of ethnographic narrative, how Jeju Island manifests the nature of the borderland and how shamanic rituals function as a voice to articulate the hidden tragedy of the island. The tragic event in 1948, in which more than 10 percent of the population was killed by the US military government, has been a deep trauma among the native islanders. Jeju shaman rituals express the trauma of the people in a very therapeutic way.

As a borderland, Jeju Island has a diverse population. Native islanders and new migrants from big cities such as Seoul practice different life styles. The land is heavily occupied by newcomers and much of it is owned by Chinese people. It is clear that the island retains deep tensions, differences, and dissonance among its residents. In this way, Jeju Island—and congruently the Jeju shaman ritual—shows borderland spirituality, which remembers hidden memories, expresses current life struggles, and envisions an end which is a joyful and harmonious feast.

Chapter 3 deals with existential aspect of border-crossing by exploring the teaching of *bardo*, the "in-between" space between death and after-death, based on the Buddhist text, *Tibetan Book of the Dead*. The imaginary borderland of the in-between is described as a space of wholeness and transformation. In the wisdom tradition of Tibetan Buddhism, souls wander in *bardo* for forty-nine days, a time that is highly violent and dangerous, yet auspicious for gaining enlightenment. This chapter focuses on the teaching of *bardo* as a border-crossing spirituality, which can be summarized as the importance of staying in the present moment and of letting go. Thus, the *bardo* teaching is a spirituality of freedom and liberation from all kinds of attachments, and of wisdom to extend the current moment fully, by being present in every moment. This teaching is annexed to the general teaching of Buddhism, the transient nature of life. To gain freedom, the wisdom to stay in the present moment is the essence of the border-crossing spirituality. In the *bardo* teaching, the best and safest guide for the journey of the borderland is a spiritual friend or spiritual mentor. This teaching of death or in-between states of life actually emphasizes the importance of spiritual friendship and the courage to stay in the present moment, moving beyond all fear or guilt that emerge from one's own projections. This chapter implies a spirituality for immigrants and more specifically for Asian immigrants in terms of application of the *bardo* teaching.

Chapter 4 focuses on the interpersonal nature of border-crossing by examining the dynamics of spiritual direction. Spiritual direction is an ancient wisdom, but is still an actively practiced ministry that goes beyond religious differences and aims to accompany spiritual seekers. This chapter examines how spiritual direction functions as a borderland where the spiritual director and the client encounter each other as "the other," and how both experience mutual transformation.

The discourse of spiritual direction has shifted from an authoritarian model into a mutual model, regarding the nature of the relationship between the spiritual director and seeker. In this model, the spiritual director's role is to open up and listen to the other, rather than guiding and teaching as a spiritual master. In today's interreligious practice, many people are willing to explore their spiritual experiences without any specific religious framework to explain them, employing various spiritual terms and practicing various forms of spirituality. Also, spiritual directors often encounter seekers from different cultures, religions, and spiritual traditions.

The seeker, as the other, will challenge and invite the spiritual director into an unknown world, which can cause fear or discomfort. The fear caused by the unknown or the other can be understood as a sheer projection of the hidden self. Thus, by embracing the other, the spiritual director can possess a deeper knowledge of him/herself. In the practice of spiritual direction, border-crossing spirituality can be delineated as radical hospitality. In the Judeo-Christian tradition, the virtue of hospitality is introduced as a way to see or embrace the Divine. Radical hospitality emphasizes the mutual exchanging of the space of the host and of the guest. In the borderland, the guest becomes a host who initiates and guides the stranger, and in accepting the exchange, the host walks into an unknown path, which promises transformation.

1

A Border-Crossing Gospel

The Healing of the Hemorrhaging Woman (Mark 5:21–34)

A NAMELESS WOMAN SUFFERING from a significant hemorrhaging illness experiences an immediate cure and, as a result, gains healing. In this story, healing signifies a liberation and transformation of her life, far beyond just her physical wellbeing. In her bold action of reaching out and touching Jesus' garment, she breaks through the demarcation line between men and women, and between health and sickness, and this border-crossing action brings her healing. This woman's story occurs in a space where the feeling of disconnect and disorder—as well as the experience of liberation and transformation—all co-exist; we call this space the borderland. In this chapter, I will explore how the healing story of the hemorrhaging woman reflects the spiritual meaning of the borderland and examine the spirituality of the border-crossing suggested by this story.

STORY AS BORDERLAND

The borderland is a space where boundary crossings occur, with different socio-political and cultural elements encountering one another and resulting in creative new situations. Often, there arise dissonance, ambiguity, and conflict. But from this chaotic situation, unexpected creativity bursts forth and, in that sense, the borderland can be a space of empowerment and transformation. This section explores the Gospel of Mark chapter 5 (New Revised Standard Version), as a whole, and the story of the hemorrhaging woman, in particular.

The Setting

The geopolitical setting of Mark chapter 5 manifests the notion of the border through the scope of Jesus' movement, which emphasizes border-crossing. According to the narrative, Jesus and his disciples cross back and forth across the lake twice, moving between the territory of the Jews and that of non-Jews. This may indicate that the story is set in a border town. Chapter 5 begins, "they came to the other side of the sea, to the country of the Gerasenes."[1] Scholars have debated the real location of the Gerasenes and have concluded that it could be in any area of the Gentiles.[2] Additionally, the narrator uses a variety of vocabulary to emphasize the notion of border or border-crossings in this passage. Although the NRSV and various other versions of the English Bible use the phrase "the other side" as the translation of the Greek word *peran* (πέραν), this word's original meaning is "crossing the border."[3]

According to the narrative of Mark 5:21–34, the second border-crossing occurs when the people of the Gerasenes ask Jesus to "leave their neighborhood" after he heals the demoniac by sending the pigs into the lake. Here the Greek word for the neighborhood is *horion* (ὅριον), literally meaning the boundary. Thus, this sentence

1. Mark 5:1 NRSV.
2. Mann, *Mark*, 278.
3. Thomas, *Hebrew-Aramaic and Greek Dictionaries.*

can be comprehended as the residents of Gentile territory asking Jesus to cross the boundary/border.[4] As such, this request can be interpreted as an action of unbelief, which is one of the themes of Mark's Gospel. However, it could also be understood as the residents' hostility (or at least lack hospitality) toward strangers, especially as they had caused serious economic disadvantages for the residents. Very often, biblical narratives ignore the responses of Gentiles who encountered Jesus, focusing instead on the Jewish rule or the response of the Jewish people. However, like any border-crossing, the one taken by Jesus causes a great amount of suspicion, discomfort, and tension, both to the Jews as well as to the Gentiles.[5]

Here, Jesus' action of border-crossing parallels his healing. Thus, the feeling of un-ease toward the border-crossing is amplified by dramatic healing. The frequent border-crossing actions, including miraculous healings, match well with the vivid and dynamic tone of Mark's Gospel, which conveys the theme of the Kingdom and power of God.

It is also remarkable that Jesus, as a border-crossing person, performs miracles both among the Jews and the non-Jews.[6] For example, Jesus feeds a crowd of five thousand in the Jewish territory (Mark 6:35–44) after sending the Twelve into the world and hearing of the death of John the Baptist. Similarly, Jesus also feeds another four thousand after serving non-Jewish people through healings (Mark 8:1–10). In chapter 5, Jesus heals the possessed man in Gentile territory and, as a parallel, he heals the hemorrhaging woman and the twelve-year-old girl in Jewish territory. The geopolitical effect of crossing over between Jewish and non-Jewish territories, along with the adept use of vocabulary regarding borders and/or border-crossings—such as "the other side" and "cross

4. Ibid.

5. Regarding Jesus as a border crosser, the narrative of Mark's Gospel is much smoother, as compared to other Gospels, especially Matthew's Gospel, which shows traces of redaction as a way to dilute the impression of a border -crosser. See Alonso, *Woman Who Changed Jesus*, 243–46.

6. Elizondo, *Future is Mestizo*, 68.

the lake"—emphasize the notion of the borderland and the action of border-crossing.

Composition

Chapter 5 of Mark's Gospel is composed of three different stories, each of which also exists in the other synoptic Gospels, emphasizing the notion of border-crossing. But in comparison, the Markan narrative—in general—and chapter 5—in particular—seems more brisk than the other two. The Gospel of Luke similarly compiles the three stories into one chapter as Mark does, but here, the importance is given to the territory of the Jews. For example, in Luke 9:40, the narrator describes that Israel waited for Jesus, and he returned. This description gives the reader the impression that Jesus is a traveler whose home is in the Jewish territory. The word, "return" is repeated three times in the chapter, thereby focusing more on coming back than on the border-crossing action itself. But the narrative of Mark is quite distinct, as it describes Jesus as a border crosser who simply moves and crosses over frequently. In this sense, Jesus resides in a borderland or a space in-between.

Matthew's Gospel is the most distinct in the composition of these three episodes, describing Jesus' Jewish identity. The healing story of the demoniacs is located in chapter 8, where Jesus begins his healing ministry after he descends from the mountain. Jesus is portrayed as the Rabbi, the teacher, and his teaching on the mountain is an important parallel to Moses who had received the Law on the mountain. Just after the teaching on the mountain, the narrator describes Jesus' healing stories as a part of his teaching, or as a clue to his identity as the true Jewish teacher.

Further, although in Matthew's Gospel, Jesus' healing is not limited to Jewish territory, chapter 8 also does not include any healing of women. The healing stories of the other two women are located in chapter 9, after Jesus calls Levi. In this way, Matthew's Gospel does not construct these different episodes as a set of border-crossing narratives. When compared to the literary composition of Matthew and Luke, chapter 5 of Mark clearly shows its emphasis on the theme of border-crossing in terms of ethnicity and gender, as well as on Jesus himself as a border-crosser.

Literary Structure

As a set, the three healing stories of chapter 5 have a literary structure that includes characteristics of a borderland: organic, chaotic, and disordered. The first story is about the healing of demoniacs (Mark 5:1–22), the second is about the healing of a twelve-year-old girl (Mark 5:23–25 and 35–42), and the third, which is inserted into the second story, is about the healing of a hemorrhaging woman (Mark 5:25–34). These three dissonant and different healing stories seem to have been dropped into chapter 5, creating a sense of disorderliness.

Regarding the length of each story, the allotment is very unbalanced. The first story takes up half the chapter, making the literary structure seem less systematic and more organic. For the content of the first story, Mark's Gospel is quite different from Matthew's Gospel, which is quite simple and without details (Matt 8:28–34). Most scholars agree that the author must have collected oral traditions of this healing story.[7] Through its long and detailed narrative, Mark's version of the first healing story (the possessed man) implies that any reader can become a witness. In terms of form, this story of the demonic man seems to have at least two different episodes: the healing story and the villagers' unbelief. The healing story manifests the characteristics of the borderland of being vivid, disordered, and organic.

The organic structure is further amplified in the second story (the girl) by the interruption and in this way, this pericope demonstrates the nature of the borderland. C. D. Marshall argues that the literary styles of the stories clearly differ, since the narrative of the raising of Jairus' daughter is written in the present tense with the frequent use of *kai* (καὶ), meaning "and," whereas the healing of the woman is written in the aorist and imperfect tenses with many

7. Mann, *Mark*, 277.

particles.[8] Thus, it is evident that these two stories, presented in the intercalated style, present different literary forms.

The intercalation style, called the "sandwich style"—wherein a narrative is generally begun, interrupted, and then resumed—gives an accommodating nature to the text, as presented in this pericope as 5:21–24—[5:25–34]—5:35–43, in which the story in the bracket is the healing story of the hemorrhaging woman. This technique serves to create suspense and to either contrast one narrative with another, or to interpret one narrative through another.[9] Usually, the inserted or misplaced the story is considered less authentic. For example, the story of the woman caught in adultery in the Gospel of John has often been considered suspicious and is even believed to be misplaced in John from the original place of the Gospel of Luke.[10] Most texts of John's Gospel make the whole story of the woman caught in adultery merely parenthetical. But in this pericope, the story of the hemorrhaging woman is neither minor nor subject to the story of the two others. Rather, the story of the hemorrhaging woman, the bracketed story, connects the two healing narratives in chapter 5. This displaced story has a central role in this structure, and this sandwiched format clearly shows the characteristics of a borderland.

If we chart this complex literary framework, it becomes clear how the story of the hemorrhaging woman—as an inserted story or a story which exists in-between the cracks of the one story—becomes the centerpiece of the whole chapter.

It goes as follows:

8. Marshall, *Faith as a Theme*, 92.

9. Donahue and Harrington, *Gospel of Mark*, 18.

10. Park, *Hermeneutic on Dislocation*, 112.

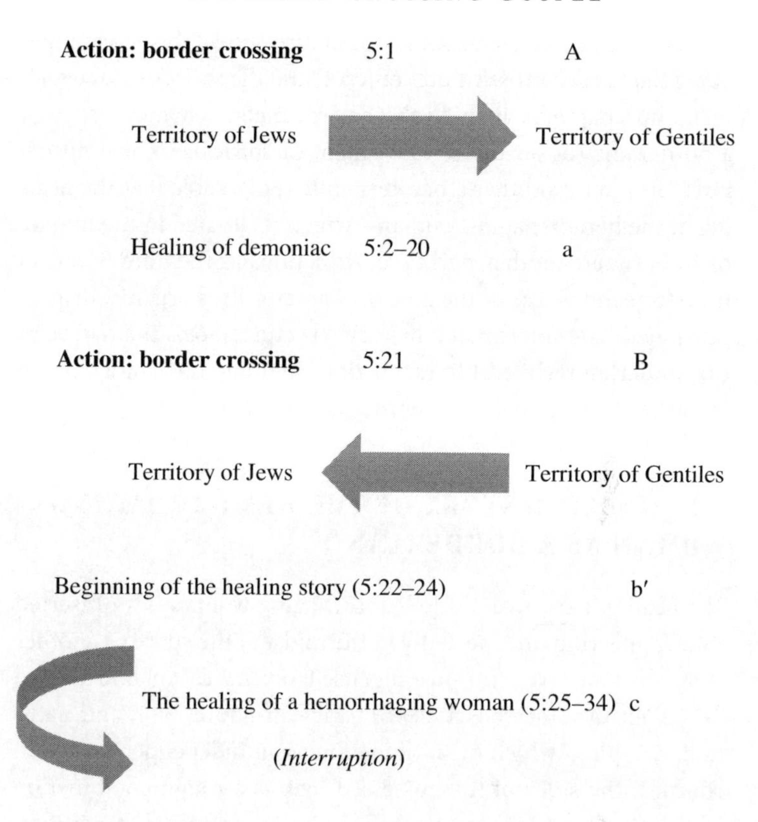

Chapter 5 is composed of two border-crossing actions between Jewish and Gentile territories (A and B), and the healing stories are introduced after the narrator describes Jesus' border-crossing actions. Thus, it can be read as A-a (Jesus' border-crossing action and healing and B-b (Jesus' other border-crossing and healing). However, the structure becomes more complicated when story b is interrupted by story c. On the way to the house of the religious leader of the Jewish community, the narrative is interrupted by another story. Literary analysis demonstrates that story c, the story of the hemorrhaging woman, has an important place within the whole narrative in chapter 5.

As we can see, the literary structure shows this story flows along the border-crossing acts of Jesus, and the three stories which make up chapter 5 include the heterogeneous characteristics of a borderland, as an uneven allotment of stories and an unusual interruption by another story. It is quite remarkable that the healing of the hemorrhaging woman—which is situated in the middle or in-between another narrative—functions as the borderland in this story and works as the core of chapter 5. This organic, disproportioned, and intercalated literary structure shows the nature of the borderland while, at the same time, inviting the hemorrhaging woman's story to be the center of this literary set.

THE HEALING STORY OF THE HEMORRHAGING WOMAN AS A BORDERLAND

The healing narrative of the hemorrhaging woman is an inserted story, appearing unexpectedly in the midst of the space of another story. In fact, even the healing itself occurs as an unexpected event. Yet the story has a clear literary structure, plot, and natural flow—all of which help it function as an independent story. In contrast, the story of the possessed man is a rough combination of the fragments of two or three episodes from oral traditions. As well, the healing story of the daughter of Jairus lacks a strong narrative power because of its disruption by another story. As such, the hemorrhaging woman's story reinforces and enhances the transformative meaning of the healings that can happen in a borderland.

Centerpiece of the Borderland

The story of the hemorrhaging woman functions as the centerpiece of chapter 5, linking together the other two stories. First, it is related to the story of the possessed man in terms of social exclusion. That first story begins with an emphasis on the possessed man's geographical dislocation and societal exclusion, with the following descriptions: he lived among the tombs (Mark 5:3); on the mountains and among the tombs he was always howling and bruising himself (Mark 5:5); and he had often been restrained with shackles and chains (Mark 5:4).

The narrative presents the man as almost non-human, using the verb "howling," which indicates the crying sound of a beast. In the Greek text, the verb used is *krazoun* (κράζων), which is the croaking sound of ravens, along with crying or crying out, and the invoking of the name of a Greek god. In the Greek world, *krazou* (κράζω) has a particular religious significance in the context of a demonic. Similarly, this word was also used in magic, being closely related to incantations, by stressing the voice of the witch like the belling of hounds, the howling of wolves, the hooting of the howl, and the hissing of the snake.[11] Therefore, according to the NRSV translation, the word "howling" insinuates that the man was not like a normal human being but more like a beast, and his situation was deeply related to a demonic state.

Also, through the description in vv. 3–5, the narrative reinforces that the man is dislocated and excluded from society. Here Mark's narrative specifically emphasizes a single man's loneliness and alienation (whereas in the narrative of Matthew, the demoniacs were at least a pair). After the healing, Jesus (in v. 19) remarkably commands the man to go back to family and friends, rather than answering his request to go wander with Jesus as his disciple; the affirmation of the healing is the return home. The man's suffering has been exclusion, and the final solution or affirmation of the healing given by Jesus is that he can again belong to the community.

The hemorrhaging woman also experiences serious exclusion and dislocation, with her alienated status clearly manifested at the very space where the healing happens. Usually, in the Gospel of Mark, the healing of women happens in domestic and private domains. When a woman approaches Jesus for healing, the location is relegated to inside the house or building. Of course, most people

11. Kittel et al., *Theological Dictionary*, 898–89.

who were brought to Jesus for healing were likely men, although it was not impossible to bring women.

But the hemorrhaging woman's healing story is located at the space in-between the public and private, as the healing occurs on the *way* to the house of Jairus. Here, the expression "on the way" indicates that it was a process and in the midst of movement. This space is the realm that negates "this" or "that," "public" or "private." To understand the spatial setting of the hemorrhaging woman's healing story, we must understand that it exists in the territory of a borderland. In other words, she was dislocated and the situation itself of being dislocated will be a source for her transformation.

Like the man who was possessed by demons, the hemorrhaging woman was excluded and alone. In her narrative, unlike in other healing narratives, we do not hear about any family or friends. Actually, kinship was one of the main social networks in ancient societies. In fact, sometimes the whole city gathered at the door (Mark 1:33) when the sick were brought to Jesus. Or in the case of the curing of the deaf man (Mark 7:32) and that of the blind man (Mark 8:12), the sick person was brought by an impersonal 'they.'[12] However, the hemorrhaging woman, with no social networks, stood alone in the crowd, mirroring the dislocation and exclusion of the demoniac.

Also, the story of the hemorrhaging woman is strongly related to the story of the daughter of Jairus, who had died or was dying and was resuscitated by Jesus. Both of them were dying and, for that reason, supposedly set apart from the society. Although the girl had not been socially excluded for a long period of time, her sickness or near death indicates that she was forcibly separated from people, which implies her vague status of in-between, between life and death. But Jesus ignores all those who argue that the girl did not "belong to this world any more," and asserts that she is merely "sleeping." While people are mourning over her death, Jesus asks her to get up, which can be interpreted as a command to return to life. Jesus further commands people to give her something to eat, as a way to affirm that she belongs to this world. Hunger can

12. Pilch, *Healing in the New Testament*, 67.

be an absolute sign of being in this world. Thus, the story of the girl deals with the status of being in-between, ambiguous, and vague.

The hemorrhaging woman's suffering parallels this girl's wandering between the living and the dead. The woman suffered from a blood related gender-specific illness for twelve years and the girl is twelve years old, an age where womanhood is burgeoning through menstruation.[13] As the text indicates, the hemorrhaging woman tried to find healing using all the money she had, but she was slowly dying of the long-standing disease. This implies that she has been heavily sick and possibly between being alive and dead. Annette Weissenrieder argues that the number of weeks, months, or even years are seen as signs of the intensity of the illness and of the imminence of death. If a physician diagnoses a patient as being near death, treatment is abandoned and the patient is already considered somewhat dead.[14] Thus, this woman's death is not as drastic as the girl's, but these two female characters share the demarcating line between the living and the dead.

The girl and the woman are also tied in relation to menstruation or blood in the context of the purity code. According to the codes of Leviticus 15, an abnormal discharge of blood caused ritual impurity and blocked access to the temple. However, Lawrence M. Wills questions if this impurity actually was ritual impurity, as it was an issue in the area of Galilee.[15] The Levitical purity code would only have applied to the woman if she were a Jew, but not if she were a Gentile.

Scholars make assumptions that the hemorrhaging woman was Jewish, offering some socio-political, and cultural symptoms[16] in relation to her disease and, as such, emphasizing that Jesus as the savior liberated Jewish women from the purity code.[17] However, there is nothing to confirm that she was a Jew. Marie-

13. Miller, *Women in Mark's Gospel*, 57.

14. Weissenrieder, *Image of Illness in the Gospel of Luke*, 253.

15. Wills, "Introduction and Annotations on Mark," 70–71.

16. Weissenrieder, *Image of Illness in the Gospel of Luke*, 253–55.

17. Dewey, "Gospel of Mark," 470–509. Also see Brock, *Journeys by Heart*, 83–84.

Eloise Rosenblatt critically points out that the text only explains that Jesus crossed the border and that there were large crowds. In other words, there is no indication that the crowd was ethnically homogenous.[18] As a matter of fact, the borderland is a land of diversity and differences, and it is plausible that the hemorrhaging woman's ethnic identity is meant to remain ambiguous and unknown. That way, her ethnic ambiguity can function as a bridge between two different ethnic cultures in the narrative of chapter 5.

The possessed man and the hemorrhaging woman share the common characteristic of being alienated and alone. The man's social status is almost like a beast or non-human being, while that of the hemorrhaging woman is hidden or invisible in a crowd. As well, the daughter of Jairus was alienated from her group because of her in-between status of being alive and dead, and the hemorrhaging woman was likely alienated by her status in-between the living and the dead. Therefore, the hemorrhaging woman's story is located at and functions as the borderland in terms of exclusion and dislocation, beyond the border between Jewish society and Gentile society, and between the living and the dead. Further, her ambiguous ethnic identity reinforces the meaning of the borderland.

The Healing Process of the Hemorrhaging Woman

The borderland is the space of "in-between" which allows conflicts, violence, and chaos caused by border-crossings. Chapter 5 of the Gospel of Mark, and specifically the story of the hemorrhaging woman, shows the characteristics of the borderland, various levels of border crossing, and particularly that of healing. The healer seems in this case to be Jesus, and the healed, the hemorrhaging woman. The symptoms are the continuous discharge of blood, poverty, and social alienation, including her suffering from the loss of social network, being forgotten, and becoming invisible. Nevertheless, this healing, which happens in the borderland,

18. Rosenblatt, "Gender, Ethnicity, and Legal Considerations," 155.

shows distortion of the situation and bursts forth a new meaning of healing. Actually, the healing occurs *on the way* to the house of Jairus. The following section will examine the scope and context of healing, and the process of the healing as the border-crossing.

Healing: The Scope and Context

The meaning of healing depends on the perspective of how we understand healing and illness. Many scholars, medical anthropologists in particular, have researched various meanings of healing[19] and conclude that healing is the attempt to provide personal and social meaning in the crisis created by and embedded in a certain illness.[20] In other words, healing is a hermeneutical process between the healer and the healed in the context of a given culture.

Thus, all healing should be understood in the context of the values of a given culture. As such, in the world of the Gospel narrative, the concept of healing should be situated within the context of the values of honor and shame, societal gender-based division, inclusion and exclusion, and attitudes toward sickness in first century Mediterranean culture.[21] Regarding healing practices, there was a demarcating line between public and private domains along gender lines. In most of the healing narratives in the Gospel, the healing of women occur in the house, while that of men happen in public places such as the synagogue or temple.

In the paradigm of healing, in terms of first century Mediterranean society and Jewish culture, elements or processes of healing can be delineated as: the transaction between the healer and the healer through use of symbols and the affirmation of healing. Transaction means that Jesus' healing power affects the sick. Here, the symbols can be words, gestures, acts, and events. Jesus as a healer sometimes touches, says a word, or even has a dialogue. Each healing story in the Gospel narrative reflects the author's

19. Regarding definitions of healing, see Kleinman, "Concepts and a Model," 29–47.

20. Pilch, *Healing in the New Testament*, 25.

21. Ibid., 27.

description of Jesus' healing power in its own socio-cultural context.

In the healing of the mother-in-law of Peter, for example, Jesus touches her and lifts her up (Mark 1), after which the narrative affirms the healing by Jesus describing the action of the healed. As an action of affirmation, Peter's mother-in-law begins to serve her guests, which can imply that she was restored to her social or ministerial function. In the case of the healing of the paralyzed, Jesus has quite a long conversation with the sick person in the Column of Solomon in the temple of Jerusalem (John 5). In this narrative, the healing is related to the Sabbath law and to keeping the Sabbath, in particular. As an action of the healed, the man complies with the Jewish leader who tries to accuse Jesus, showing that the efficacy of the healing is often related to the social context in which the stories are situated.

In the story of the hemorrhaging woman, Jesus says to her, "Daughter, go in peace. Your faith has saved you," which functions as the affirmation of her healing. In Mark's narrative, a daughter not only has a social space, but also has a special meaning as a disciple. In this statement, readers can find the woman's status has been elevated to the level of a model of faith and being a disciple, as well as having regained a sense of belonging.

The Process of Healing as Border-Crossing

Most importantly, this story, in the framework of a healing narrative, includes many border-crossings in which the subject and the object of healing are switched. First, the healing action begins with *her touching his* clothes (v. 27, emphasis mine), not through Jesus' touching her. In other words, the initiative of this healing is not healer, but rather the healed.

Even in this border-crossing action, the woman's gesture is quite bold. Matthew's version refers to the tassels attached to the corners of the cloak, reminding readers of the passages of Num 15:38 and Deut 22:12, but in this Gospel, the narrative simply mentions Jesus' clothes. It is remarkable that this gospel uses diminutive expressions, such as little and few, but the narrator chooses clothing rather than the tassels. The fact that the same narrative uses the word 'clothing' emphasizes the woman's bold action. While approaching the crowd secretly, because of her ritual impurity or social exclusion, the woman's determination indicates her strong belief that mere contact with Jesus will affect a cure.[22]

Second, there is reversed transaction between the healer and the healed. Unlike an ordinary healing story, the healer, Jesus, is still very passive and just recognizes that his power has been extracted. Scholars argue that this story indicates the healing power of Jesus, which is beyond social codes and the purity code, in particular.[23] As mentioned above, in most healing narratives, Jesus is active while the healed are just simple recipients. But this story is exceptional. Through the whole process of healing, the woman functions as an agent or subject. It is she who attains the healing power; on the contrary, Jesus recognizes his healing power was transacted to someone. In fact, Jesus appears to have no control over his power. Elizabeth S. Malbon observes that the healing narrative is unique in Mark's Gospel because this woman's request is granted without Jesus' direct intention.[24] In other words, she is the one who takes action for her own healing and, as a consequence, she is empowered and experiences healing.

Third, in this healing story, Jesus takes an auxiliary role to raise her status. Although Jesus solemnly says, "Daughter, you faith has healed you," his real role is limited to affirm the healing. Thus, the woman actively achieves her new status as a disciple by being called daughter and a full member of the community, as well as a whole being who is free from sickness.

Most importantly, the woman instantly realizes that she has been healed through her bodily knowledge; she immediately feels she is cured. In fact, her subjective experience of the various stages of the healing is emphasized throughout the story in a way that is unprecedented in the Gospels. We are informed of her initial

22. Mann, *Mark*, 285.

23. Miller, *Women in Mark's Gospel*, 55.

24. Malbon, "Fallible Followers," 36.

hearing of the news about Jesus, which corresponds to Jairus' initial seeing of him (Mark 5:27); about the thoughts that motivate her approach ("Even if I just touch his clothes . . ." Mark 5:28); about her internal experience of the healing itself ("she knew in her body that she had been healed," Mark 5:29b); and about her reaction to the miracle ("fearing and trembling, knowing what had happened to her." Mark 5:33).[25] In this way, the narrative clearly shows how she was determined to make herself healed and to act out what she wanted to achieve.

The nameless woman achieves her new status of being a daughter, just as the title was also given to the little girl whose father was the leader of the synagogue. Scholars further stress the woman's achieved title of daughter, in comparison to the title of Jesus as the Son of God. Many explain that the woman is an example of a new discipleship. Indeed, she is a new member of the Christian community as well as a returned healthy member of the larger community.[26] The title of daughter given by Jesus is reminiscent of his saying that "whomever does the will of God is my brother, sister and mother" (Mark 3:35). The woman now becomes a subject and gains her authority as a disciple in her community.

BORDER-CROSSING SPIRITUALITY

In this story, the situation is a typical description of a borderland, which is very crowded, jumbled, and chaotic. Hence, even when Jesus claims that something has happened to him, the disciples respond to him saying, "in this big crowd, anybody could have touched you." Everything is hectic, and out of that situation, the woman who is not supposed to be in such a public place initiates action.

In this way, this healing story shows how a borderland dweller who struggles with exclusion and powerlessness can overcome social barriers and belong to society. First, this story shows how

25. Marcus, *Mark 1–8*, 368.

26. Miller, *Women in Mark's Gospel*, 60.

a woman's autonomous and determined action overcomes her marginalized situation in terms of gender and defilement. Here, the woman breaks social norms in terms of gender and health. Mary Douglas argues that the purity code functioned as a rule to exclude certain members, women in particular.[27] Throughout history, women have experienced certain limits and exclusions, especially as immigrants (both undocumented and documented) or as newcomers in certain cultures. Even now, immigrants and people who carry two cultures often feel doubly marginalized and excluded, from both the home culture and the host culture.

The most startling aspect of the story of the hemorrhaging woman is that she herself initiates the action to break social norms. The Japanese biblical scholar Hisako Kinukawa points out that the story begins by describing the hemorrhaging woman seven times with participles, which do not give the character a distinct personality. However, the narrative describes her action with the verb, "touched his cloak," which can mean that her active motion is the peak moment of her life.[28] Like many other women characters in the Bible, we do not know the woman's name, and only know her sickness, which maybe the source of her great shame in Mediterranean cultural standards of the first century. In her determined action, the nameless woman regains her subjectivity, personality, and dignity.

In the first healing story of the given chapter, we see no sense of autonomy. The fact that the man was possessed by demons means that he has lost his dignity, in that he cannot control his behavior and he cannot belong to society. So much so, that even when Jesus commands the demons to leave the man, the man is very passive. Similarly, in the other healing story, the twelve-year-old girl who is dead also does not act as an agent, but still becomes a recipient of Jesus' action. Jesus places his hands on the girl and commands her to get up, but the narrative does not describe what happens to the girl, either emotionally or physically. After the

27. Douglas, *Purity and Danger*, 7–28.

28. Kinukawa, *Women and Jesus in Mark*, 33.

miracle, Jesus asks people to give her something to eat, rather than the girl expressing her own hunger or needs.

Only the story inserted in the middle shows bold action on the part of the character, and it brings the woman whole being as an agent. In this sense, the story of the hemorrhaging woman is a healing story. Additionally, the woman raises her level of self to the height of Jesus, as the border-crosser. Although her hemorrhaging itself does not cross a border physically, the woman performs many other kinds of border-crossings. Just as Jesus crosses boundaries —defiling himself by talking to a man living in the impurity of a graveyard and by touching the impure body of a dead girl—the woman also surprisingly crosses social boundaries —appearing in the male domain of public space and by intentionally touching the cloak of a male. Thus, this story reveals a border-crossing spirituality, which provides autonomy for the voiceless and the outcast, and helps the woman to act as an agent.

This is all made possible by the disordered conditions of the borderland, a place that is chaotic and often overly populated. In the hemorrhaging woman story, there is clearly a crowd and confusion, amid which she approaches Jesus. In a situation in which it is very hard to say who is touching whom, the woman's hand grasps the garment of Jesus. In her desperation she tries anything, even breaking rules and crossing boundaries.

Here, healing is related to the word *dynamin* (δύναμιν), which means power. Elaine Wainwright explains in *Women Healing/Healing Women*, The Markan use of *dynamin* (δύναμιν) is associated with the language of healing.[29] In this healing activity, Jesus wonders how his power was transacted. His power passes to the bleeding woman; she receives the power. As the text suggests, she recognizes that her somatic symptoms are gone and she can stand again in the public; things have changed and she is whole.

Life itself is a borderland. In terms of socio-economy, culture, and politics, our lives can often float in an in-between state –in situations which are ambigous, unknown, and unclear. Experiences of exclusion, alienation, and invisibility are not rare in our

29. Wainwright, *Women Healing*, 113.

global multicultural society. The story of the hemorrhaging woman teaches us the wisdom of the border-crossing: that every moment should be appreciated and seized. Furthermore, her whole healing process is an embodied experience and body knowledge, rather than a cognitive process and cerebral knowledge. The woman takes bold actions which go beyond cultural norms and boundaries, and she achieves her new status of being whole, including her subjectivity. In this spirituality, being on the margin can be a privilege to practice a person's subjectivity and to gain transformation and healing.

2

A Border-Crossing Ritual

Jeju Island's Shamanic Interstitial Space

SOME BORDER-CROSSING SPACES OR borderlands are created in the process of ritual, through which participants hold a certain experience or situation that is not integrated within a person or community, and construct creative dimensions or gain new perspectives of life in relation to the situation. A well-known anthropologist, Victor Turner, describes ritual as liminal space, emphasizing the state of being ambiguous; the 'yay and nay' exist together. Turner argues that a person or a particular group who goes into the liminal state is often considered invisible and even forced to undo old patterns so as to embrace the new role that will be given in the future.[1] In this space, all participants are equal and, from among them, a new order can emerge after this liminal state.

Scholars such as Catherine Bell argue that ritual, as an anti-structure, could deconstruct existing social and emotional structures which might be forced upon people and oppress them. More importantly, in ritual practice, a person who does not own one's subjectivity could gain a sense of agency.[2] As such, ritual could

1. Turner, "Betwixt and Between," 97–110.

2. See Bell, *Ritual Theory*, 27.

empower those who experience isolation, powerlessness, and frustration so that they experience transformation in the ritual. Very often, through the imaginative nature of ritual, God and human, past and present, and the living and the dead exist together in ritual space. Also, by the ritual's performance function, people in the ritual touch, enact, and embody all memories, dreams, and hopes.

As a case study of border-crossing spirituality, I chose a shaman's rituals on the island of Jeju in South Korea, where I performed field research from 2011 to 2014. Jeju Island maintains the nature of a borderland in the geo-political and cultural sense. Congruently, Jeju shaman rituals reflect the island's culture and history, which comprise the contents, emotions, and environment of the ritual. Also, the shamanic ritual creates or provides a transformative response to Jeju's geo-political borderland situation. In this sense, the shaman's rituals that I examined indicate borderland spirituality, in presenting a past that was forced to be silent, signifying that the present is accepted as is, and projecting a harmoniously-embraced future.

I found a fascinating concept of middle space or in between space within the Jeju shamanic ritual called *Miaji Bengdi*. In the Jeju dialect, the phrase *Miaji Bengdi* signifies an empty space between this world and the other world, which is paved with nothing but pebbles. In *Miaji Bengdi*, transformation happens. Here, symbolically, souls with deep angst and wounds that cannot leave the world become ready to leave for the other world, and the remaining people no longer feel troubled. As a borderland, Jeju Island itself is the *Miaji Bengdi*, the space for learning a new emerging spirituality of friendship, social justice, and creativity. In this chapter, I describe how the island has become a borderland through a brief ethnographical sketch and examination of the Shamanic ritual, *Kut*, in which the shaman creates a borderland space, an in-between space where transformations occur.

AN ETHNOGRAPHIC SKETCH OF JEJU ISLAND

On a hot afternoon in June 2012, I landed at the Jeju International Airport, which was very crowded with international tourist groups, as well as Koreans enjoying their summer vacation. The weather was very hot, humid, and windy, which is typical of summers on the island. On the second floor of the airport, I found a fancy coffee shop with free Wi-Fi, but at the same airport there is also a modest snack shop that sells street foods such as ramen (instant noodle), skewered fishcake, and *kimbab* (Korean sushi) at cheap prices. It was fascinating to see old and new styles of food places together in the same international airport.

Outside the airport, while waiting for a ride, I heard various languages such as Chinese, Japanese, English, and Jeju dialects (which are quite different from any other Korean dialects), as well as various Korean dialects. Merchants speak various languages, according to the customers' needs, but islanders recognize one another as insiders and often charge different prices than for outsiders or tourists.

On the street, palm trees stand against the strong winds, expressing a tropical feeling, and traditional stone statues of Jeju's grandfather (its mascot) stand on the ground, in contrast to the modern buildings. Beside traditional markets, luxurious modern department stores have sprouted. On this volcanic island, the middle mountainous area is filled with various coffee shops and amusement parks, and along the ocean are residential houses and open fields.

The houses and the fences around the houses are beautiful and unique because they are made of black basalt stone, left from an era when there was no cement but which have mysteriously stood firmly against the fierce winds of Jeju Island. Yellow Youchai flowers look astoundingly beautiful against the dark stone fences.

Jeju now has a great number of immigrants from the cities of the mainland, South Korea, including celebrities and artists. These groups show great interest in creating a new cultural landscape and are eager to learn the history and culture of Jeju Island. In

2013–2014, I met a group of new arrivals studying Jeju's shamanic tradition with a native scholar. These immigrants from the mainland are drawn by the island's natural beauty and the cost of living, which is far lower than any other big city in South Korea. Also, there are special foreign language schools that teach in English only, so some families move down for these educational benefits. These groups are creating a new pattern of consumption—including food, fashion, and travel—which is more urban in style. One result is that Jeju's traditional natural dyed clothing has become a popular and expensive fashion trend on the mainland.

Jeju was created by a volcanic eruption; in the center of this island is Mt. *Halla*, its spiritual home and the birthplace of its founding myth. The name of the highest town within Mt. *Halla* is *Youngsil*, which literally means the house of spirits. Between *Youngsil* and the flatlands is a freeway that meanders through a forest. But because the town in the forest was totally destroyed during the *Sasam Sageon*,[3] one of the most tragic events of this island, the road is now home to a number of entertainment parks and fancy restaurants. Here and there, one can see monuments erected to comfort the souls of the victims of the *Sasam Sageon*. In the middle of the island, there is the beautiful *Sasam* memorial center, which shows how the tragedy was silenced in the anti-communism ideology.

On the ground level of the island is a farming field of tangerines, which is one of the main crops of the Jeju people. Since the 1970s, Jeju Island's tangerine farming has provided economic stability for the islanders, along with tourism. In this agricultural area, most people still maintain the traditional way of living by working in the fields.

Along the seashore, many hotels and restaurants are owned by the Chinese and serve for Chinese tourists. In 2012, there were big complaints by Jeju islanders to the governor, who gave foreigners permission to purchase real estate. In fact, there is tension between people who want to keep Jeju Island as a part of Korea and others who want this island to be an international city. However,

3. Details of this tragic event are below.

most ordinary Jeju islanders only express or articulate minimal concern. International hotels and resorts continue to grow, offering tourists activities such as golf and horseback riding.

Along the tourist resort area, there is a small town called Kangjeong. On the day I first visited the town, I found almost five hundred people protesting the construction of a naval base there. Since 2007, this small town has struggled for eco-justice and for clean water in the area, and rejected any possibility of war or military activities. This protest now has attracted international attention, and people have continued the protest, proclaiming Jeju as "Peace Island."[4]

The protest has been led by the Catholic Church and individual activists. Daily Mass is celebrated in front of the construction zone and the participants sing and dance as a way to peacefully protest the construction. The police have arrested priests and religious women who demonstrate on the construction site, but they have continued this fight for seven years. In an interview, Fr. Jeong Hyun Moon, one of the movement's lead organizers, says, "There is no guarantee we can stop this construction, however, we must safeguard this place from militant movements which will destroy nature."[5]

Jeju has become a new place where people from various backgrounds, cultures, and religions can live together, sharing concerns of social justice and eco-justice through the peace movement. Many activists promoting justice and peace from cities have even migrated here to support this movement.

However, tension exists, as local islanders are split between those who agree with the naval base construction and those who do not. Traditionally, Jeju Island was highly communal and exclusive of outsiders, so that this conflict has caused a high level of tension and discomfort among the islanders.

When I arrived, I recognized that Jeju islanders were suspicious of outsiders wanting to study their island. So it was when I

4. Ko et al., *East Asia and Jeju*, 15–18.

5. Jeonghyun Moon. Personal interview with the author. Seoul, South Korea, July 15, 2014.

finally befriended a native islander scholar, Dr. Moon, that I found it far easier to study the culture of the island, both in general and of rituals of shamans in particular. They call the family-like ties among the islanders *Kuendang,* and once I was received into the circle of friends, then everyone wanted to help my research. Walking around Jeju Island, I found that the old and new, peace and violence, and local and global realities—these various elements all exist together as a borderland.

JEJU ISLAND: MULTIPLE ASPECTS OF THE BORDERLAND

Jeju island includes multiple aspects of the borderland. Historically, the island has been considered unimportant and the islanders have experienced exclusion and oppression. Culturally, the island shows a unique culture, compared to the culture of South Korea; it is a borderland. The island has developed a female centered culture and an anti-hierarchical mind. The myths of Jeju goddess manifest the women-centered mind of Jeju islanders. Also, geopolitically, Jeju island manifests characteristics of the borderland where marginality creates an alternative perspective. Jeju island, having been discarded, might become a center of a new emerging culture.

Historical Aspect of the Borderland

Throughout its history the island has been a borderland, both as a periphery and a margin. Jeju's identity is more than Korean and carries multiple identities, including an independent identity as Jeju people. The most widely known name of the island was Tamra, which was renamed Jeju in 1211 when it surrendered to the Korean dynasty. As a matter of fact, Jeju literally means far away from the peninsula. Even the name Jeju itself objectifies the island as the other. Recently, local scholars have proposed returning to the name Tamra as a way to emphasize the autonomy and identity of the island.

However, as a borderland, Jeju Island can be a frontier to receive other cultures through the seaway. Jeju professor Namlin Hur argues that the island can be considered a frontier area from the perspective of the South Asian Pacific Sea. Very often, the history of Korea was written from a view that focuses on the Eurasian continent and connects China-Korea-Japan. Jeju Island, which historically has the character of being periphery and frontier, has existed as the borderland.

Through its history, the island suffered from exclusion, alienation, and exploitation as the borderland. In terms of loyalty, the islanders looked suspicious to the mainland, which charged overly heavy tributes from which some islanders escaped. As a harsh response to islanders who leave the island, the government promulgated the law to ban them from leaving. Many were incarcerated on their own land, suffering from exploitation and injustice.

Jeju Island was an independent country, functioning as a center of Pacific cultural encounters and with highly developed sailing skills in the ancient period,[6] but which in the seventh CE was colonized by one of the ancient kingdoms of Korea. Finally, in the twelfth CE, the Joseon dynasty named this island "Jeju," and asked islanders to start paying heavy tributes as a colony. According to records, Jeju Island had to offer precious seafood caught in the deep sea through hard work by women divers. These women divers, called *Haenyeo,* worked naked, vulnerable to the cold water and risking death from their diving work.

The exploited history of Jeju Island continued, when it became a colony of the Mongols. Even now there are several customs, such as raising cattle, strong shamanic rituals, and Buddhist practices brought from Mongolia. Also, some Mongol people stayed and married Jeju women, and their descendants—as well as descendants of people from Vietnam and Taiwan—comprise the Jeju population.[7] This history and hybridity of the Jeju islanders manifest the nature of the borderland. After Mongolia left the island, the Joseon dynasty continued to control Jeju.

6. Cheon et al., *Reinterpretation of Jeju History*, 276.

7. Ju, *Journey on Jeju Island*, 403.

Although Jeju belonged to Korea as of the fifteenth CE, the island was still considered marginal and of least importance. The island was a place of exile for dangerous and disloyal elites; for the mainland, Jeju was a land of forgotten people and social death. This island has had a long history of exploitation and exclusion and, because of this, has developed a sense of community among the islanders and hostility toward the mainlanders.

In the twentieth CE, Korea underwent much tragic history, but the Jeju islanders experienced particularly severe events. Especially, *Sasam Sageon*, or the "April 3 Incident" in Jeju was a tragedy that resulted in the largest number of victims, after the Korean War, in the modern history of Korea. *Sasam Sageon* (April 3, 1948–September 21, 1954) left nearly 30,000 people dead, almost 10 percent of the population of Jeju Island, and many others had to leave the island. These thousands of civilians were killed by the joint forces of the army and the police from the mainland, working under the United States Army Military Government in Korea (USAMIK). The right wing that allied with USAMIK killed islanders who disagreed with them or fought against them, accusing them of aligning with Communists.

The backdrop for the *Sasam Sageon* is complex, but it can be summarized as follows. First, the Jeju islanders experienced severe alienation and exploitation by the mainland. Their resistance against Western colonial powers existed against the cruel demands of the Japanese imperial government, as well as the Catholic Church of France. There was a series of resistance riots and a strong call for independence, which came out of a need to protect themselves from outsiders. Their accumulated resistance against outsiders stirred up their sense of urgency and competency, and was channeled against the US military government.[8] Second, Jeju Island was labeled "Red Island" by an extremist right wing group and the US military government. Jeju was considered suspicious and even traitorous, and this label provided a justification for the violence against the civilians of the island. Third, the US Army adopted a policy to establish a barrier against communism on the

8. Cho, "Pastoral Preaching in Jeju Island Churches," 81–85.

Korean Peninsula. However, on Jeju, the leftists received strong support from the people, and this situation created a desire to be independent.

In this context, the police shooting of demonstrators on March 1, 1947 ended in an eruption of violence. The leftists on Jeju were forced to make a choice between either submitting to the USAMIG or resisting them. Toward those who did not cooperate, the US military government commanded the "Scorched Earth Strategy," which killed the civilians and destroyed the land.[9] More tragedy followed, with the Jeju people divided and distrustful of each other in the midst of confusion and turmoil; this caused a large and lasting scar on the islanders' hearts. Further, outsiders from the mainland exploited the islanders, resulting in strongly critical feelings against the mainland.

To make it worse, the government was ruled by military dictatorship, which embraced the cold war ideology, and banned Jeju islanders from speaking about *Sasam Sageon*. But during and after the tragedy, many Jeju people who had been exiled to Japan created a diaspora community that was able to maintain the unique identity of Jeju islanders.[10] After the liberating grassroots and democracy movement against the military dictatorship in Korea, Jeju islanders requested that the hidden story of the *Sasam Sageon* be revealed and, in 2010, the president of Korea officially apologized for the event.

However, it is not easy to wipe away the wounds of the tragedy. Almost every family on the island experienced trauma and lost family members, including the thousands missing. Even within households, family members hurt each other and created wounds by not saying anything to one another.

Jeju Island historically has been a borderland, with experiences of isolation, exploitation, and exclusion. Now the people of Jeju are demanding to keep their home as Peace Island, emphasizing that the island not be used for any military purposes. This is the core of Kangjeong's demonstration of the naval base construction,

9. Park, *Truth of Sasam Sageon*, 57.

10. Ibid., 67.

to ensure no further violence. The Jeju people desire to keep peace of the island and to mourn the suffering they have already endured. They have erected towers in villages that lost entire populations and have offered shamanic rituals for the victims.[11] These shrines attract visitors to the island, but more importantly, the islanders continue to reconcile among the Jeju people at these shrines.

Cultural Aspect of the Borderland

Jeju is called the "Island of 18,000 Spirits," holding a unique and distinctive culture, including customs and language. Because of its distance from the mainland and its history of isolation, Jeju Island kept their old traditions intact.[12] The nature of the borderland manifests in their culture, which is creative in subverting the patriarchy and men-centered order.

Recently, feminist scholars have begun to have interest in the myths of Jeju Island, in which the world of gods is very much female-oriented. Jeju scholar Youngsu Yang argues that the gods in the world of Jeju myths exist as parents of human beings who are fairly harmonious with and obedient to the gods.[13] Also, most of the gods were human beings first, who, after a distinct and adventurous life, became gods. In fact, the stories of gods are mainly composed of their adventures as human beings. Thus, the story of these gods are very human and these gods want to act as helpers of the Jeju islanders. In this land and in the story of gods, women have more power than men, and in this way, myths of Jeju subvert the patriarchal order. Jeju Island has a strong feminine tradition in that women have more voice and power in all aspects of life, and this is expressed in the stories of female gods.

Unlike Korea's male-centered folk traditions, Jeju Island holds myths of goddesses. These stories are recited at shamanic rituals in Jeju, and in this way, this oral tradition remains intact.

11. Cho, "Pastoral Preaching in Jeju Island Churches" 110.

12. Hur, "Jeju's Historical Topos," 27.

13. Yang, *Jeju's Myths in the World*, 57.

In analyzing these stories, the female gods show more characteristics of boldness, intelligence, and sexual power.[14] According to the founding legend, Jeju was created by *Mago Halmang* (*Mago* Grandmother; goddess). In this story, *Mago* created the island by carrying mud in her apron then dying by slipping into the pot of hot soup, thereby giving her flesh to her five hundred sons. This story shows the mercy of the goddess who created and nurtured the people on Jeju Island.

On the island, there are many goddess stories that emphasize women's subjectivity and independence. For example, the goddess of destiny, Lady *Gamungang,* expresses her independence from her parents. According to the story, *Gamungang*'s father asks three daughters what motivates them to live in this world. The first daughter says that she lives for the father, and the second daughter lives for the mother. Finally, the third daughter, the protagonist, replies that she lives for her genital power. Because of this reply, she is kicked out of her home and begins a new life, finding a husband and teaching him about sex.[15] This woman, who opened up her own destiny, becomes the goddess of destiny. The story of *Gamungan* shows how the male-centered social order is vitiated.

On the mainland, Confucianism formed the social order in which the male has more dominant power and females are considered less important and complementary, rather than independent. Also, women's sexual power is considered dangerous and suspicious and the value of women's sexuality is measured and appreciated through the eyes of society and, very often, of the male.[16] *Gamungan*'s story emphasizes the autonomous sexual power and sex of the female as a source of life energy and destiny.

Similarly, the female god *Jacheongbi* demonstrates woman's creativity and boldness. The Lady *Jacheongbi* goes to a well and meets a man named Moon, with whom she falls instantly in love. She becomes determined to be his lover and so disguises herself as a man, accompanies him on his way to study, and lives with

14. Moon, *Jeju's Shaman Dance*, 67.

15. Kim, *Goddess*, 165.

16. Lee, "Menarche," 88.

him as a colleague. They even sleep together, but Moon does not notice *Jacheongbi*'s gender. But after three years of study, she takes him into her house and marries him. However, after the wedding, Moon goes to heaven (his hometown) and forgets *Jacheongbi*. So she takes a trip to heaven to claim him as her husband. She endures some trials and is eventually given permission to be Moon's spouse by the king of heaven, who asks her to remain in heaven as a goddess. But she wants to come down to Jeju Island with seeds of grains to feed its people.[17]

This unusual story of *Jacheongbi* shows the female energy of desire, which includes determination, wisdom, and boldness. Very often, people feel uncomfortable with women's sexual desire; it is difficult to find any literature expressing women's sexual desire.[18] Interestingly, this young woman wanted to have a man from heaven, and she underwent trials and adventure to achieve all that she wanted. Her will to keep her man and her wisdom in winning the trials reflect how Jeju islanders consider women and gender equality.

Jeju Island has many shrines to worship local deities. In the Songdang area, there is a shrine dedicate to a god couple. In this shrine, people offer more wine and fruit to the wife god than to the husband god. This shows how much women deities are respected and loved by Jeju islanders.

The world of myth is congruent with the Jeju society and Jeju culture, which resist the main culture, in which women do not have a sense of subjectivity. On this island, women have more economic power. While men do some work, women take care of the farming, rearing of children, and cooking. Because the males went to sea and often died, women took responsibility to care for the family. Especially, the women sea divers catch and provide the basis of their diet, seafood such as abalone and sea cucumbers. In the cultural aspect, Jeju Island shows clear characteristics of a borderland in which the gender roles are switched and women have more power.

17. Kim, *Goddess*, 121.

18. Tolman, "Daring to Desire," 101.

Geo-Political Aspect of the Borderland

Geographically, Jeju Island is a kind of borderland, the marginal site of the Korean mainland. But at the same time, this island is an entry port from other countries such as Japan, Taiwan, and China. Because of this geo-political location, Jeju can be counted as a borderland.

On my field trip of 2011–2013, I saw that the island looks very much like a Western-styled tourist town. During the vacation months of July and August, there are numerous Chinese tourists, and most people who work in the tourist industry on the island speak Chinese. However, Jeju Island has had a long and close relationship with Japan. Because of its geographical proximity, many Japanese come to Jeju for sex tours, food, and hunting. Even today, there are many places on the island where Japanese is spoken and people have direct connections with Japan. Also, historically, many Jeju islanders were exiled to Japan, and the city of Osaka has a Jeju diaspora community. In my observations of shamanic rituals, I found many Jeju people have family members who live in Japan, doing manual labor and experiencing severe discrimination.

Recently, the town of Kangjeong has become the central place where various groups of people gather, constructing a borderland from which people make an effort toward eco-justice and peace. As pointed out above, the location of Jeju Island—from a military perspective—can be central in defending East Asia's Pacific naval power, controlling China and aligning with Okinawa, Taiwan, Guam, and Hawaii. However, because of the ecological destruction threatened by the construction of the naval base, many peace movement activists from all over the world have gathered together on Jeju. In particular, Jeju Island has proposed peace movement called Pax Asiana, which promotes collaboration with other Asian countries rather than being initiated by one strong country, to seek eco-justice and non-violence.[19]

In the summer of 2014, I experienced many people collaborating for the goal of peace. The Catholic Church of the Jeju

19. Ko et al., *East Asia and Jeju*, 43.

Diocese has gathered a faith community where two priests reside permanently and peacefully rally against the construction. In addition to the priests, some religious women have also volunteered to live there and have joined this peace movement. Every day on the street, they offer daily Mass and prayer, and various groups of people gathered from beyond the island participate in dancing and artwork as a movement of resistance.

A special event of this movement is a peace march that occurs in July. People from all over Korea participate in this march, gathering together in Kangjeong. They talk and perform folk art, and dance the indigenous dance, guided by various groups, composed of both non-native and native Jeju islanders.

In this geopolitical landscape, Jeju Island demonstrates a new cultural reality as a borderland. This situation of Jeju is dissonant in terms of their identity and affiliation, but also full of new energy that is highly creative. Every different aspect of the various groups brings different relationships with the island. This brief history of the island is sketched out as a way to examine the nature of the borderland of Jeju. Some critics explain the situation of Kangjeong as quandary of South Korea's loyalty—between its military ally, the United States, and its main trade partner, China.

SHAMANIC RITUAL IN JEJU ISLAND

The Jeju people show a strong desire to offer public shamanic rituals every April 3, for the souls of the victims of the *Sasam Sageon*, to guide them to the other world, restoring peace, and letting go of the angst.[20] In general, shamanism in Korea has been degraded as superstition and considered a "less civilized" native religion than Buddhism, Confucianism, and Christianity. However, in Jeju society, the shamanic ritual has been claimed a cultural root and spiritual identity. In 2013, on the 65th anniversary of the *Sasam Sageon*, a *Kut* was held in the port to console the souls. As a public *Kut*, this shamanic ritual is *Haewon SangSaeng Kut*, which means

20. Park, *Sasam*, 25–41.

a resolution of the *Han* (angst and a deep feeling of sadness) of the victims and mutual transformation between the living and the dead soul.

For this *Kut*, Dr. Moon Moobyong wrote a poem:

> Souls! Discharge long and unpolluted sadness on the thorn tree
> Which stands on the edge on this world, *Miaji Bengdi*.
> Go! Cry and go lightly like a butterfly.[21]

Here, the *Miaji Bengdi* means an empty field where the living and the dead souls encounter each other and where unresolved emotions and sadness are held, until the souls are finally let go into the other world. Dr. Moon explains that the space of the *Kut* ritual is *Miaji Bengdi,* where the forgotten history is restored, and the sad souls and the remaining family experience healing and reconciliation.[22]

The shamans on Jeju Island—unlike those in other parts of Korea—feel no shame in their vocation. Because the shaman works for the village where the shaman was born, she is deeply related to her neighbors. As a family member or friend, the shaman knows already the issues of clients. Also, the scale and expense of the ritual is much smaller than for rituals on the mainland.

In the structure of the Jeju *Kut*, three segments are essential: welcoming the souls, encountering the souls, and making a way to the other land. In the welcoming section, the shaman calls all the names of sprits, including the souls of the *Sasam Sageon*, the ancestors of the Jeju islanders. In this ritual, the shaman invites the souls of any Jeju people who have died at sea, died in the *Sasam Sageon*, and died in wars. After welcoming the spirits, the shaman invites all sprits to sit.

Then, the shaman enacts the souls of those who want to speak to the family or to any other attendants of the ritual. Anthropologist Yongjoon Hyun and other scholars explain this nature of the

21. Mubyong Moon, *A Poem Dedicated to the Souls of SaSam Sageon* (poem, recited at Kimnyung sea port in Jeju, April 13, 2013).

22. Mubyong Moon, "4.3 Trauma and 4.3 *Kut*" (paper, National Academic Conference on *SaSam Sageon*, Jeju University, April 29, 2011).

shaman as "pseudo possession," which signifies that the shaman is not totally possessed by spirits.[23] At this moment, the shaman becomes highly creative as a hybrid person who understands and conveys the emotions and statements of the spirit, yet it is the shaman who interprets the message.[24] In every shaman ritual, the delivery of the message is one of the most therapeutic and healing parts. A shaman who knows her client's concern and the family's history enacts as the spirit who promises to resolve the concern; the shaman understands how the spirit feels about the client.

Also, in this state, the shaman sends a message to the living people, family or relatives in most cases. The shaman Soonsil Seo, who performed the *Sasam Kut,* said:

> I see the darkness and deep frustration of the soul who was buried at sea and no one could find them. It was sad and frustrating. I did my best to let them go peacefully and connect with all the living Jeju people.[25]

As a way to communicate with the souls of the victims of the *Sasam Sageon,* who died in the deep sea, the shaman walked into the water and danced in the water.
Seo further stated, "I am so proud of performing a ritual through which we wish numberless souls of victims to go peacefully to the Western land." In this annual ritual, a different shaman is chosen each year, depending on the place where they perform the *Kut.* The Jeju islanders choose a place where many innocent people were killed and the shaman who lives in the area serves the ritual.

However, in private rituals, souls from the *Sasam Sageon* are always remembered. Because more than 10 percent of the islanders were killed, in almost every family ritual, the souls who lost their lives in the *Sasam* are invited. When I observed a personal healing ritual of a person in back pain, the souls of the victims of the *Sasam* were also invited there. When the presiding shaman called the

23. Hyon, *Jeju Musok Yonku*, 56.

24. Park, *Hermeneutic on Dislocation*, 154.

25. Soonsil Seo, personal interview with the author, Jeju Shaman Institute, July 20, 2014.

souls of her family, these souls were invited and remembered. The shaman expressed the fear and anger that the souls experienced and the family in the ritual remembered the painful family history and cried together.[26]

In Jeju rituals, people prepare good food to entertain and console dead souls, including the souls of the *Sasam Sageon*. With music, dance, and soulful dialogue with the dead, this ritual visualizes the borderland in the segment called *Gilchiki*, which literally means to make a road to the other world. In every Jeju *Kut*, the *Gilchiki* part visualizes the empty space of *Miaji Bengdi*, where the third space is located in between this world and the other world. In this space of ritual, forgotten historical moments are remembered, pouring out deep emotions and accepting the present as it is, including letting go of sadness and helping the soul go to the other world, and finally embracing the future in a harmonious way.

In this segment, people bring a big plate (8" x 24") to symbolize the middle space, the *Miaji Bengdi*. The shaman wears a costume as the guardian of death who guides the soul into the other world. Onto the plate, the shaman enacts gathering weeds with a scythe, and picking up pebbles that could bother the soul when crossing the border between the living and the dead. Then, using bamboo sticks, the shaman makes 10 rows of arches, through which the souls must pass. When the shaman walks through these arches herself, her assistants spread paper butterflies, which symbolize the transformation into a new being. As a way to visualize the purification process of the soul, shamans dance and the gathered people pray for the souls to be cleansed of resentment. When the shaman passes the first row and moves into the second one, people kneel on the ground and offer bills of money for the journey. Once the shaman completes to move into the second row, the first row of arches is cleared away.

In the last row of arches, shamans put new clothing so that the dead souls can take off their old clothing and put on new ones. In Korean popular religion, new clothing for the soul symbolizes

26. The *Kut* was performed at the *Kut* house in Jeju on July 5, 2014 and ended on July 6, 2015.

transformation. After this segment, the shamans throw the clothing that soul takes on into a fire.

The ritual itself is the *Miaji Bengdi*, but this segment is time for letting go. The shaman dances slowly and cries in front of the final row of arches. All the family members also cry. In the mind of the shamans and of participants who know this cultural enterprise, this moment is the time to let the souls go to the other world. After this segment, the shaman brushes the client's body, as a way to draw a boundary between the living and the dead. As a final gesture, the shaman spreads red beans on the floor and all the participants leave the ritual space. I believe it symbolizes the closing of the borderland space.

After this segment, the people come back to the ritual space to eat lunch and dance together. At this time, the food is shared with everyone. For public rituals such as *Sasam Kut,* the event continues afterwards as a festival. In this way, there is no division between friends and enemies, insiders and outsiders, or foreigners and fellow countrymen.

BORDER-CROSSING SPIRITUALITY

Three years of fieldwork on Jeju Island with its shaman rituals has shown the border-crossing spirituality which occurs in the borderland. As a borderland, Jeju island continues to maintain ambiguity and paradoxical realities: Old myths of goddesses breathe while, at the same time, international tourism grows; it maintains a strong sense of family, but at the same time, newer immigrants are constructing a community, through which they are eager to learn the unique Jeju culture and tradition; Jeju has long been considered the margin or periphery, but can also be seen as the entrance to the Pacific ocean and a global center for a new Asian Pacific economy; and most interestingly, at this global destination and gathering place, shamanism is highly respected and performed, and exists complementarily with other Western religions.

The vibrant energy of creating the future and the tension between unresolved wounds add to Jeju Island's identity as a borderland. Despite the dissonant voices of the old versus the new, one tangible thing unites the Jeju people—the *Sasam Sageon*. People remember their loved ones and the forbidden history of the tragedy through the shamanic rituals, in an organic way. Whenever persons or families sponsor a ritual, which essentially invites their ancestors, they meet the souls who died innocently and brutally at the hands of the military government. Since the government's officially apology, the Jeju islanders have begun to work openly on memorializing the history and creating meaning.

In the shamanic ritual, the whole history is recited, through which female goddess stories are heard. Stories of brave, wise, and bold women are told and their spirits are invited to the ritual. There, all kinds of emotions are expressed, such as fear, anxiety, and frustration. Shamans who know their clients' life struggles express them in front of the spirits, including those of the ancestors. In this borderland space of ritual, shamans often cry for the clients, or for the spirits, or for both. Clients cry too, and this part is very emotional. Even as an observer, I could not stop crying while listing to their life stories and the stories of spirits. The ritual is open for anyone to pour out their emotions. Here, people can feel a sense of reconciliation and reunion with the souls and self.

Then, this ritual enacts a process of letting go of the souls. Using the large plate, all the participants envision the empty space through which the souls go to the other world, in peace and without any resentments or attachments. At this moment, paper butterflies symbolizing purified and enlightened souls, are strewn on the ground. Then through the shaman's motions of building a road to the other world, the souls and the participants are separated again.

In Jeju rituals, or the borderland space, the memories that were too violent to be verbally expressed, are actualized. Memories that could not find language are articulated and expressed through dance and chants. Also, current life struggles, including emotions, are also articulated. When a person is able to create a narrative, that person can have perspective on the experience of the life struggle and, presumably, find transformative meaning in the struggle and then create actions to move forward. Actually, in the Jeju shaman ritual, a shaman who knows her clients on a deep level can articulates in their stead what they cannot express or articulate for themselves. As well, the shamanic ritual creates a vision for the future that is more harmonious with all, including blessings of the dead souls and gods. After sending away the spirits, the participants enjoy a feast. The feast is almost an apocalyptic joy, with dancing and singing, and where no one is excluded.

In its protests against the naval base and in its rally for peace, Jeju Island functions as a borderland. In this movement, people from various geographies and religions become unified. In this vision, they practice the shamanic ritual, perform grassroots dance, and play music. However, it is clear that the island retains deep tensions, differences, and dissonance. Yet without a domineering power or absolute dogma, Jeju Island—and congruently the Jeju shaman ritual—shows border-crossing spirituality, which remembers hidden memories, expresses current life struggles, and envisions an apocalyptic hope, which is a joyful and harmonious feast. In this borderland, many people gain new identity as Jeju islanders and participate in creating a new culture.

3

A Border-Crossing Journey

Reading the Tibetan Book of the Dead

LIFE IS TRANSITIONAL, BECAUSE life is on the move. Although human beings seek stability, each moment that composes life is transitional. Thus life itself is borderland, existing on the edge. There are many spiritual teachings in Buddhism that demonstrate how to live in the moment. One specific teaching of Tibetan Buddhism elaborates borderland spirituality by talking about death.

Tibetan Buddhist texts articulate certain periods of time between the moment after death and before rebirth called *bardo*. However, the word *bardo* literally means gap, and, thus, the word signifies a state of being *in-between*. It can indicate the interval of the moment of death and right after, or it can include any in-between time while living.[1] The *bardo* designates a situation of being neither this nor that. Perhaps it signifies being both this and that, or even more than a sum of this and that.[2] The *bardo* encapsulates the meaning of borderland spirituality, which addresses a space to experience fear of severe violence, as well as one of great opportunity to gain liberation and freedom.

1. Trungpa and Rinpoche, "Commentary," 1.
2. Bhabha, *Location of Culture*, 35.

Fundamentally, Tibetan Buddhism teaches that in the moments after death the soul resides in an empty space. According to Huston Smith, the "in-between" of the past and the future is so close to a mathematical point that it seems scarcely to exist. Yet, paradoxically, it is everything in being, and the only thing we directly experience, for the past is gone and the future has yet to arrive.[3] The text *The Tibetan Book of the Dead*,[4] thus, deals with the space between the moment of death and rebirth, opening up great possibilities to gain wisdom and liberation, while implying the same possibility in one's living situation.

This chapter first provides a general introduction of the content and history of the text, then examines the text as literature, paying special attention to the literary structure, style, rhetorical devices, and sensory symbolism. Then, finally, it suggests an interpretation of this text as a showcase of borderland spirituality from the perspective of a first generation Asian immigrant woman. In analyzing the literary structure of the text. I use the version of Francesca Fremantle and Chögyam Trungpa, to which many critics give credit, in that they follow the original meaning of the Tibetan text.

GENERAL INTRODUCTION

According to Tibetan wisdom, there are six *bardo* states: the time (a) between birth and death, (b) the meditational state, (c) the dream state, (d) the moment of dying, (e) the interim between death and rebirth, and (f) the process of rebirth itself. A human being experiences life as the space between birth and death (a), which means the time span of one's whole life in this world; (b) and (c) indicate prayer and dream when the human mind submerges into sub-consciousness or unconsciousness. Nevertheless, the boundary of each state of *bardo* is very blurry and interstitial.

3. Smith, "Introduction," xiii.

4. From this point on, "the text" refers to *The Tibetan Book of the Dead.*

Fundamentally, Tibetan Buddhism considers death as a process of the whole life. "The prayer of 'the Six *bardos*'" exemplifies the way a soul should fill the moments of life given: 1) when the *bardo* of birth is dawning upon the soul, it should study, reflect, and meditate without falling into laziness; 2) when the *bardo* of dream is dawning upon the soul, it should unify and sleep, and practice prayer by controlling dreams; 3) when the *bardo* of meditation is dawning upon the soul, it should be firm in the practice of meditation and visualization without falling into the power of confused emotion; 4) when the *bardo* of the moment before death dawns upon the soul, it should enter into clear awareness of the teaching without any attachment; 5) when the *bardo* of between death and rebirth, dharmata, is dawning upon the soul, it should recognize every vision as sheer projection; and 6) when the *bardo* of rebirth or becoming is dawning upon the soul, it should strive to prolong the results of good karma, without jealousy.[5]

During the period of *bardo* that begins at the moment of birth and finishes at the time of death, every human being should make efforts to study, reflect, and meditate on the essence of life. As a process or result of the way the person is striving to live awake, all six *bardo* states can be understood as an opportunity to achieve awareness or enlightenment or liberation, although the text pays attention to only the *bardo* between death and rebirth.

Content

The Tibetan Book of the Dead, as a part of a series of *bardo* teaching, is about the experience of death. The text deals with the duration of forty-nine days from the moment of death to the period of rebirth. In East Asian culture, heavily influenced by Buddhism, the forty-nine days after a soul's death are considered sacred, and many rituals are offered for the soul. The text strongly stipulates to recite it during forty-nine days and offer rituals for the dead

5. Fremantle and Trungpa, *Tibetan Book of the Dead*, 98.

person, explaining what happens to the dead after breathing has stopped.

The Tibetan Book of the Dead consists of three parts of *bardo*: recognition of the primordial luminosity at the moment of death, recognition of the true nature of peaceful and wrathful deities, and recognition of how to prevent rebirth.[6] The first *bardo* is for one who gained enough spiritual wisdom and practice. Only the person who recognizes the emerging light as the nature of emptiness at the moment of death will gain liberation. The person who does not embrace the light, or even gets frightened by it, wanders into the next stage of *bardo*, the truth of *bardo* or *tharmata*.

This second stage of *bardo*, the truth of bardo, *tharmata*, takes the central place in this teaching. This is called "*bardo* as it is." The text indicates that the reader of this text should tell the soul how to interpret the visions that will appear. The first part of the truth of *bardo* is about the manifestation of light of the five Buddhas, each having its own color, manifesting direction, which represents wisdom. According to the text, the light is overwhelmingly bright, so that the soul easily gets frightened, and that is the reason why the reader tells the soul that the light is the wisdom of Buddha. Each Buddha's compassion functions as a hook to help the soul enter into the Nirvana, while the consort of each Buddha assists from the behind the soul to be hooked.

Unless the soul recognizes the nature of this vision, the second part of this *bardo* unfolds. This *bardo* is more scary and fearful because each Buddha appears in a wrathful appearance at this time. The essence is that the scary form itself can be a revelation of the Buddha nature, and indeed it symbolizes the compassion of Buddha nature. Also in this stage of *bardo*, whenever the brilliant light of color appears, the dim and soft light appears simultaneously. This dim light symbolizes the six realms that people should avoid falling into, which are realms of hell, gods, humans, beasts, jealous gods, and hungry ghosts. These six realms represent the eternal place where the soul suffers from extreme unhappiness, eternal goodness, pride, greed, jealousy, and discontent. In the

6. Neumaier-Dargyay, "Buddhism," 97.

Buddhist teaching, even the world of gods, which is spiritual bliss, is vanity. The soul who gets scared of the brilliance of the light becomes strongly attracted to this dim light.

The third part is about the *bardo* of becoming, which deals with fragments of memory from past lives, and the way the soul's emotional response to these memories lays the foundation for the emerging next life.[7] Here, more dramatic scenes, such as hounds hunting down the dead and blinding blizzards making the soul run for shelter, appear to the soul. Also, the text recommends that the soul let go of any emotion from the past as a way to be free from this visualization. If the dead cannot take this advice, judgment by Yama, the god of death, appears. In the Western medieval portrait, there is an angel holding a scale of the evil and good actions during the life in front of the gate of Heaven. Likely, here is the final judgment, but instead of the scale to measure the evil and good actions, the dead person faces the mirror that shows what he or she did, and the hangman appears to persecute the dead soul. It is scary, and almost a dream-like experience in that the soul sees its own persecution. The given teaching in this situation is that even though the soul suffers from death, the death or pain is not real, but a projection of the mind. Once the soul recognizes that the experience is a sheer projection of its mind, the soul gains liberation.

If the soul still does not gain freedom, then the image of a couple engaged in sexual intercourse appears. The soul should try not to be engaged emotionally in this scene as a way to prevent its rebirth. If the soul is attracted to the woman, and repulsed by the man, it is reborn as a man, and vice versa. This recalls the concept of the Oedipus complex.

The Tibetan Book of the Dead, in conclusion, mentions that a spiritual friend or companion should read it to the soul, so that the soul is reminded of the teaching even when it faces great fear of death, and, as a result, recognizes the wisdom of Buddha, or emptiness, and gains liberation. Here the importance of spiritual friendship or spiritual companionship is emphasized.

7. Ibid., 99.

The History of the Text

The Tibetan Book of the Dead is one of the spiritual texts that crosses national and cultural boundaries, and challenges or deepens hidden aspects of life, especially by focusing on the state of death. In 1927, this book was translated by Lama Kazi-Samdup and edited by W. Y. Evans-Wentz through Oxford University Press, and since then it has evoked extraordinary interest among various Western intellectuals. Well-known scholars of religious studies such as Huston Smith, as well as the spiritual leader of Tibetan Buddhism, the Dalai Lama, have written lengthy forewords for this text. However, scholars such as Eva K. Neumaier-Dargyay explain that this teaching is very limited to certain traditions, and that this text has not been considered an authentic religious text.[8] That said, along with its popularity in the Western society, today many classes are offered on this text through the Nyingma tradition of Tibetan Buddhism.

In Tibet and the border areas of the Himalayas, this text has been used as a ritual guidebook for the dying and their relatives and friends, and as a meditation book for the living. At the age of seven or eight, a novice monk begins to study this text, memorizing the whole of it. With his master, the young monk is supposed to visit a dying person as a part of his study. In this way, the student experiences the embodied notion of death and the impermanence of life, one of the Noble Truths.[9] As Glenn H. Mullin accurately points out, contemporary Western society negates death, which is a part of life, by not talking about it.[10] In this context, this text is countercultural and challenging, yet at the same time enriching Western culture in a spiritual way by helping readers to face and study the reality of death and of life. This book is not only to help

8. Ibid., 96.

9. In Buddhism, the Four Noble Truths signify that life is suffering, the cause of suffering, the cessation of suffering, and the gain of Nirvana through the middle path.

10. Mullin, *Death and Dying*, 4.

the soul to gain freedom from fear of death, but also for the living to achieve wisdom.

A Scholar of Tibetan Buddhism, Harold Coward, explains that *The Tibetan Book of the Dead* is one of a series of instructions on six different types of liberation from rebirth: liberation through wearing, through seeing, through remembering, through tasting, through touching, and through hearing.[11] This text focuses on listening as a key component of liberation.

There are various teachings of *bardo* based on oral traditions. According to Lama Lodru, the first stage of *bardo* is primarily for those advanced in the meditation to achieve liberation, while the second stage of *bardo* is primarily for ordinary people; the English translation of *The Tibetan Book of the Dead* pays much attention to the second *bardo*.[12]

It is believed that Padma Sambhava composed the book, and it was written down by his wife, Yeshe Tsogyal. Scholars guess that it was written in the late eighth century.[13] However, Padma Sambhava is a semi-mythic figure who, according to the legend, hid the text in Gampo Hill in Central Tibet. The hidden text was later discovered in the fourteenth century by Karma-Lingpa, who belonged to the Nyingma tradition.[14] The text belongs to a type of Tibetan revelation literature classified as a treasure text, which fulfills the requirement of having been discovered later and the author's having been given a canonical status. This text passed through various redactions, and finally in the seventeenth century, Rikdzin Nyima Drakpa redacted the corpus of rituals and teachings.[15] In the tradition of Tibetan Buddhism, a treasure text has special esoteric power in that anyone who reads or hears it without question gains liberation as a benefit.[16]

11. Coward, "Jung's Commentary," 261.
12. Lama Lodru, *Bardo Teachings*, 34.
13. Thurman, *Tibetan Book of the Dead*, 83.
14. Fremantle and Trungpa, *Tibetan Book of the Dead*, xii.
15. Cuevas, *Hidden History*, 186–200.
16. Fremantle and Trungpa, *Tibetan Book of the Dead*, xvi.

This book is a guidebook or a travelogue of the after-death states, designed for ordinary practitioners, to help them undergo the process of death smoothly.[17] This reading can result in illumination for the soul. Even though the text does not set certain requirements for readers, many lamas warn that they will need to learn this teaching through meditation as well as devotion.[18] According to the tradition of Tibetan Buddhism, the person who initiates the Tibetan path (Vajrayada) takes a higher position to enlightenment than do scholars and leaders in any other tradition, such as Mahayana or Theravada Buddhism.

LITERARY EXAMINATION

This section examines the literary style, structure, rhetorical devices, and the sensory symbolism of the text. The literary texture demonstrates the aims and the goal of the text, as well as conveying the message of the text very effectively.

Literary Style

In the introduction, Francesca Fremantle and Lama Trungpa state, "This [book] 'Great Liberation through Hearing,' the means of liberation in the *bardo* for meditation practitioners of average capacities, is in three parts: the introduction, the main subject-matter, and the conclusion."[19] As a guideline, this book includes rubrics for the reader who is helping the soul's transmigration. Upon reading the text, readers easily can find rubrics such as "reading loudly this part three times."

The main body of the book is composed of the first part (the Chikai *bardo*), the second part (the Chonyi *bardo*), and the third

17. Rinpoche, *Tibetan Book of Living and Dying*, 106.

18. Very often, Tibetan Buddhist schools require students who want to study the teaching of *bardo*, the Tibetan Book of the Dead, to recite mantra 100,000 times for initiation.

19. Ibid., 1.

part (The Sipai *bardo*). Each part begins with a message supposed to be given to the dying person. For example, this is the entry to the first *bardo*:

> O son of noble family, listen carefully without distraction. . . . O son of noble family, you will experience three *bardo* states: the *bardo* of the moment before death, the *bardo* of truth and the *bardo* of becoming. Of these three, the luminosity of *dharmata* in the *bardo* of the moment before death shone until yesterday, but you did not recognize it, and so you had to wander here. Now you will experience the *bardo* of truth and the *bardo* of becoming, so recognize what I will show you without distraction.

This quotation shows that some part of the text assumes the role of summary of what is happening to the soul as well as introduction to the next stage.

Also in the beginning of the text, there are marks of "The method of instruction" and "The time of instruction." These parts in the introduction suggest who should read the text, and when this text should be read, according to the physical condition of the dying person. The text clearly shows the characteristics of a manual, although later this rubric-like nature begins to be blurred with the description of the *bardo* content itself.

It is very clear that this book is not just for intellectual understanding of the *bardo*; the text often suggests the reader invoke prayer, emphasizing the importance of remembering the mercy and compassion of the Buddha nature. The text itself indicates that its reading process should always begin with an elaborate offering to the Three Jewels (Dharma, Buddha, and community) and be followed by certain prayers:

> recite *Inspiration-Prayer Calling on the Buddha and Bodhisattvas for Rescue* seven or three times and recite loudly the *Inspiration-Prayer for Deliverance from the Dangerous Pathway of the Bardo* and the *Main Verses of the Bardo* as a preparation for reading '*The Great Liberation through Hearing*' seven or three times.

Here, the suggested numbers three or seven function as universal symbols for perfection and fulfillment. This book certainly is written for a reader who guides the soul and, in so doing, the reader embodies the teaching of *bardo, not diminishing spiritual merits of the contemporary readers.*

Literary Structure

Analysis of the literary structure reveals the plot of the text clearly. This book shows a "v"-shaped structure, and the crucial message of the whole text is located at the lowest point, showing a parallel between the first and the third; and the first half contains the last part of the second *bardo*.

Reading the text, the reader easily recognizes that this structure has a different way of ending and beginning from that of Western literature. In the main body of *bardo*, the text teaches the first *bardo*, which happens just after death. After that, the text continues the teaching of the second *bardo*, which has the central place in its meaning. However, in the portion of the teaching of the second *bardo* about manifestations of blissful deities, the text proclaims the first half of the teaching is over. Then, the second half begins with the wrathful deities of the second *bardo* stage.

This structure can be drawn as a "V" shape, as below:

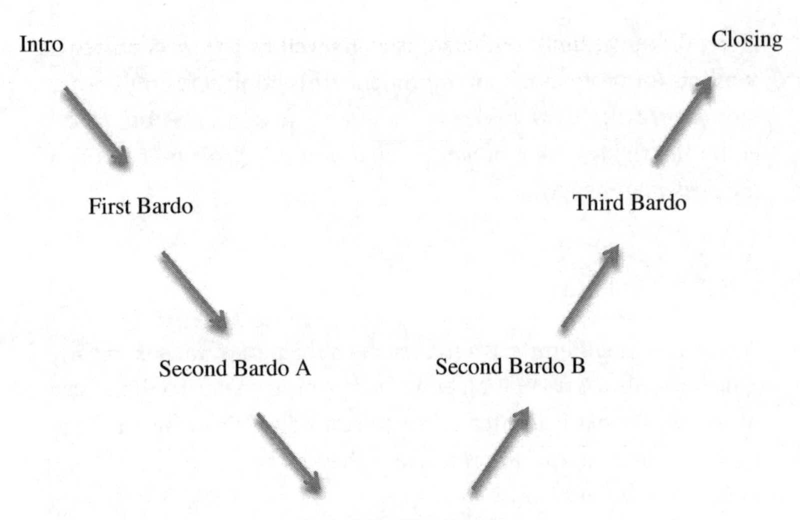

This structure strongly conveys the core message, the importance of the "in-between." Actually, the part that composes the End of the First Part occupies just three lines, but the text stresses this part by using a different editing style and font. The segment, which is dangling at the end of first part of the second *bardo*, the teaching of blissful deities, does not include much content. In other words, the part itself manifests the core teaching of *bardo*, the in-between space, and the text wisely enough shows the importance of the in- between space of *bardo*. In this analysis of the literary structure, the meaning of the *bardo* as the *in-between space* is strongly emphasized.

After this first part of the second *bardo*, the journey of the soul will be more tumultuous and dangerous. In the last part of the second *bardo*, the text describes 58 wrathful deities, and emphasizes that it is not easy to understand the empty nature of reality through the wrathful deities and to recognize that these horrifying deities come from one's own mind. In other words, the mind is more fearful than before and awareness is weaker, yet at the same time, the mind is not distracted at all. Therefore, the state of mind has a high opportunity to gain liberation.[20] In this way, this text

20. Mullin, *Tibetan Book of the Dead*, 206.

stresses the meaning of *bardo* itself, as well as the importance of the mind's awareness.

Rhetorical Device

The rhetorical device used to convey the message effectively in this text is repetition. Repetition can function as a tool to remind the dying or dead souls where they are situated in this journey. In the case of persons who studied and read the text during their lifetime, their souls easily comprehend where their stage is now. Even those who are not familiar with this teaching can follow the guidance easily because of the repetition.

Also, repetition functions as an implement to underscore the importance of certain messages. Repetition as a rhetorical device functions as an amplifier of the meaning of the text, which emphasizes the importance of studying and practice during life, and of understanding of all phenomena as human projection.

For example, the phrase, "Do not be afraid, it is just your inner projection," is repeated almost every place in this text, with some variation. Death itself could be accepted, but the process of dying causes lots of fears. This text fully understands that the human condition and the reality of death are sources of fear.

Also, the repetitive phrase, "projection of mind" is very provocative. The text emphasizes that all the phenomena that the soul experiences are sheer projections of the mind. In this text, the knowledge that every scary image is the mind's work, or that of projection of the mind, reflecting the soul's attachments to the past, such as joy, resentment, anger, etc., helps the soul to gain detachment and in so doing, liberation.

Especially in the second part of the *bardo* of truth, the soul faces most terrifying images of wrathful deities. According to the text, even scholars or teachers cannot escape the terror and intensive fear caused from this scene. However, this text stresses the importance of the realization that every horrifying image is a production of the soul's own mind. When the text describes the image of a wrathful deity such as Heruka, who has three heads and six arms, and wears skulls, the text also adds that it is like a stuffed lion.

Through reading this text, readers naturally get used to the repeated expressions that embody the crucial teachings of emptiness. But at the same time, the listener or the soul supposedly gets to know or be reminded of the teaching of *bardo*. Through this repetitive pattern, the text imposes the meaning of the journey of the *bardo* not only on the soul, but also on the reader, and, more importantly, imposes on both the importance of the process to achieve liberation.

Sensory Symbolism

The Tibetan Book of the Dead is very strong in sensory expressions regarding sounds, color, light, and imagery. In the second *bardo*, the text continuously describes the color of the light, which manifests the Buddha's wisdom aspects. The text explains the symbolic meaning of color and light in this *bardo* stage. In this stage, the soul experiences the brilliant light, which causes a deep sense of fear. However, all things are empty and nothing, and once a soul remembers the fundamental teaching of nothingness, it achieves liberation. Otherwise, the soul continues in the state of *bardo* or something even worse. The soul that walks into the dim light falls into one of the six realms which endlessly continue karma.[21]

By three or four days after death, if the soul does not achieve liberation, it will wander in the land of the second *bardo*. At this stage, the soul recognizes itself as one who wanders in the *bardo*, although the psycho-physical body and intellectual mind of the soul are not the same as before, even though the soul might feel no different. Here the seven stages of blessed deities vividly and strongly stress the symbol of color.

21. Six realms represent the psychological eternal state of being, which includes realms of gods, humans, jealous gods, hungry ghosts, beasts, and hell, caused by karma. Interestingly enough, in Tibetan Buddhism, even the state of gods, which represents bliss of goodness, including desire for prayer or spiritual cultivation, is not the ideal state of being, in emptiness.

In the first stage, Buddha Vairocana, who represents the wisdom of Dharma, appears with his consort in the brilliant blue light. Also, there is a dim white light, which represents intentional ignorance.[22] If the soul chooses the dim white light, it falls into the realm of gods, and if the soul escapes from the blue light, it continues the journey of dangerous *bardo*.

In the second stage, the brilliant white light appears, and the revealed Buddha is Vajrasattva or Aksobhya. Brilliant white represents the element of water, and symbolizes the realm of complete joy. At the same time, there is a dim smoky light, which represents the realm of hell. The text explains that the karma of anger causes this dim smoky light. If the soul is scared of the color of brilliant white and walks into the dim smoky light, it falls into Hell or the state of paranoia. If the soul did not embrace the bright color, it continues the journey.

In the third stage, yellow light comes, and the revealed Buddha is Rinchen Jungne, who represents the element of earth. At the same time, a dim blue light emerges, which symbolizes the human realm, and signifies the essence of pride and the source of passion and mental disturbance. Although the color yellow is so overwhelmingly bright that it causes fear, the soul that has meditated on the Buddha nature can grasp the brilliant light. If the soul cannot achieve realization that everything is empty, it continues the tumultuous journey of *bardo*.

In the fourth stage, Amitabha Buddha appears in brilliant red light, which symbolizes the element of fire, as well as compassion. If the soul cannot follow the brilliant red light, perhaps because of the influence of its bad karma, it falls into the realm of hungry ghost. If the soul does not embrace the bright red light, it continues the journey of the *bardo*.

In the fifth stage, Amoghasiddhi Buddha comes in green light, symbolizing the element of air, as well as accumulated good actions. At the same time, a soft red light of jealous gods attracts the soul.

22. Lama Lodru, *Bardo Teachings*, 25.

In the sixth stage, the six brilliant colors, which symbolize the Buddha wisdom, will appear like a rainbow along with the dim or soft colors, which symbolize the six realms, all together. These strong colors of white (wisdom of emptiness), blue (mirror-like wisdom), yellow (wisdom of equality), red (wisdom of discernment), and green (action-accomplishing wisdom) are parallel to soft white (gods), soft red (jealous gods), soft blue (human beings), soft green (animals), soft yellow (hungry ghosts), and soft smoky light (hell). The text explains this stage as the chance to be liberated into the wisdom of emptiness by realizing Buddha nature.[23]

In the seventh stage, the same five colors appear in terrifying forms of Dakini, which symbolize the feminine energy of either destruction or creation. Often, the image of the Dakini is angry, dripping blood and wearing skulls. Also there comes soft green light, which symbolizes the animal realm, ignorance and slavery. In this text, the color of light or of deities, which symbolizes various aspects of the wisdom of Buddha, helps readers to visualize the experience of *bardo* in a vivid way.

Along with color, the description of manifestation of deities in the text is also unusual, challenging our dualistic notions. Buddhism challenges and invites a non-dualistic nature of reality through striking form. First, when deities appear, they are in a sexual embrace with their consorts. For example, in the seventh day of the blissful deities' manifestation, the Peerless Lord of dance is in sexual union with a red Dakini. This image challenges the readers who are dualistic thinkers and consider the spiritual as not sexual. Very often, however, not always, the deities have consorts, and they appear together in the form of sexual union. Sexual union symbolizes the union of body and mind, femininity and masculinity, and secular and sacred.

Second, the form of the deities, especially the wrathful ones, is not beautiful and pleasant, but rather scary and even disgusting. One of the most common descriptions of the wrathful deities is seen in that of Heruka, the visualization of masculine energy. The text describes, for example, the form of Heruka: his body is deep

23. Fremantle and Trungpa, *Tibetan Book of the Dead*, 53.

red (or blue, yellow, white, or green) in color, and he has three heads, six arms and four legs, and stands in the center of a blazing light. His hair is streaming upward, and he is laughing like thunderstorm. This image and color is often depicted in the Tibetan art of mandala.[24]

However, this text continuously emphasizes that the fearful form is indeed wisdom of the Buddha, and invites readers to learn to see the Buddha nature as emptiness and to embrace it beyond fear.

BORDER-CROSSING SPIRITUALITY

This interpretation of the text focuses on the teaching of *bardo* as an example of borderland spirituality. This view claims the borderland as a space to empower and transform the lives of immigrants who experience various socio-cultural marginalities. The person who resides in the borderland lives in the in-between space, and one of the central natures of the *bardo* is that it designates a period or space of in-between in a deep uncertainty. However, being aware of being in the in-between moment helps the person who experiences turbulence to gain greater wisdom and power.[25]

As an immigrant woman, along with thousands of other immigrants who feel dislocated, restless, and anxious, I recognize that the story of *bardo* resonates with the life situation of immigrants. Because immigrants live in a new situation, which is quite different from their native environment, they can easily become fearful and panicked. Very often, immigrants feel they fit neither in their own culture any more, nor in the new culture of the hosting country. It is common for immigrants to experience trauma and danger in the new place, and to feel challenges in settling into the new

24. In Tibetan Buddhism, the mandala is an expression of the fundamental symbol of the cosmos and at the same time, of the microcosm of the human soul. As a prayer practice, Tibetan monks draw Mandala on sands, woods, and paper. Generally speaking, Tibetan art, mandala in particular, is very colorful and vivid.

25. Rinpoche, *Tibetan Book of Living and Dying*, 108–10.

situation, in the same way that a soul wanders in the *bardo* space. In this sense, immigrants live in a kind of *bardo*, and, thus, this text invites them to live their difficult life in a creative way.

In the border-crossing spirituality, immigrants who feel dislocated need to find a creative and transformative answer as to how they can engage creatively with self, other, and God in order to be empowered. The teaching of *bardo* in Tibetan Buddhism can provide a path to such a border-crossing spirituality.

Let us elaborate the spiritual meaning of *bardo*. First, *bardo* teaching invites immigrants to stay in the present moment. *Bardo* means a state of being between two other conditions, and the best way of living in this situation can be explained as the immediate experience of now-ness.[26] Francesca Fremantle explains the concept of now-ness as one in which the past is gone and the future has not yet come,[27] and this concept can be applied to every moment of our lives. Actually, now-ness is a fundamental discipline of border-crossing spirituality. Many people who reside in the borderlands have left their homeland with good or bad memories, looking for a new possibility. For immigrants to achieve this newness clearly requires that they should understand their life as it is now. Furthermore, the dynamics between space and place form a landscape that emerges as a culture process. In this landscape, according to Eric Hirsch, the now-ness that people have in a place creates a space for those understandings.[28] Thus, *bardo* teaching invites immigrants to focus only on the present, rather than on the past or the future, and in so doing, invites them to create a space where they can feel rooted and safe.[29]

Immigrants are those who feel uprooted from their own culture. They may keep many unresolved feelings such as nostalgia, resentment, jealousy, or sadness. Very often, they carry nostalgia and resentment of being left behind in a foreign land. In the case

26. Fremantle, "Tibetan Book of the Dead for the Living," 171.

27. Ibid., 171.

28. Hirsch, "Landscape," 66.

29. Park, *Hermeneutic on Dislocation*, 3.

of Asian immigrants, their Confucian cultural background of filial piety often can prompt this kind of emotion toward their parents.

Furthermore, the immigrants who work hard in their new countries recognize that their life situation is no better than that of those who live in their homelands. Because of the rapid growth of much of Asia's economy, therefore, when immigrants visit their motherland, they often feel jealous and betrayed.

Also, Asian immigrants have a tendency to hold on to their native lifestyle within a Diaspora community. For example, if you go to Korea Town in Los Angeles, it looks almost like Korea. The residents keep their original life style, which creates a deep sense of alienation and isolation from the multicultural reality of the hosting country.

Looking at the history of Asian immigration, which began in the eighteenth century, we can see there many scars. For example, Chinese men were involved in building railroads and were treated badly by both their employers and the US government. After their labors, they had to come back to their camps like prisoners. Also, as a part of the sad immigration history, the Japanese internments of World War II left a deep scar in almost all Asian immigrants. A more recent example is the L.A. Riots of April 1992. Although the riots began against the unfair verdict of an African-American man, they expanded into riots and raiding people's property. Korean-American groups became the main target of the African-American groups. The cultural differences and success of Korean-Americans raised intense resentment towards their culture, as they were the primary targets during the riots. Koreans were considered the "model minority," as they had achieved great business success in Korea Town as owners of small grocery and liquor stores. Blacks targeted Korean-Americans, for they felt economic inequality in a nation they considered their own. Tension had been simmering between African-Americans and Koreans in Los Angeles for decades. Such conflict included the lack of the perceived exploitation and racism of the black community by Koreans, the Korean's failure to hire blacks, and the robbing and shooting of Koreans by blacks. This event motivated the Korean-American community to cooperate with other minorities, but as a cultural body, many Asian immigrants have retained a passive way of living in the society. Considering the multicultural reality of today's cultural society, the *bardo* teaching that the past should be considered as sheer memory and one should move on, embracing the now-ness, is potentially one of the most powerful spiritual teachings.

Also in the life of immigrants, the ambition for success, which is supposed to come in the future, is a big driving force. This kind of ambition causes many of them to work seven days a week without any vacation, and often compel their children to be excellent students. However, this way of life to concentrate on the future erases the emphasis on the present moment. In other words, *bardo* teaching reminds immigrants to stay "here and now," rather than being caught up in resentment of the past or ambition for success in the future.

The second teaching of *bardo* shows the importance of community or at least of relationship. At the time of death, it will be desirable to have a companion. This teaching presupposes that the human soul does not leave the body automatically after it stops breathing. According to Tibetan tradition, although a person stops breathing, she or he still keeps the relationship with the body and maintains their integrity as a person. Literally, it is the time of the "in-between," in which the person is more vulnerable and open to new possibility.

In these moments of death and after death, a spiritual friend or spiritual mentor can accompany the soul. Here in the dangerous journey of *bardo*, although the soul and the spiritual friend become one or gain a hybrid identity, neither loses their distinct life and destiny. The relationship is more inter-subjective, based on mutual friendship and trust. According to borderland theory, gaining this hybrid identity, which is a symbiotic relationship with the other, is a crucial way for the soul to achieve empowerment. Here, the Tibetan teaching of *bardo* reaffirms the power of spiritual friendship and shows an example of this hybrid identity.

In border-crossing spirituality, one of the most crucial elements is community. Without community, the people in the borderlands, or immigrant people, feel alienated, and cannot overcome their alienation. In the power of community, the resident of a borderland encounters others and creates relationship, which can empower them.

Furthermore, in the journey of *bardo* in the text, Buddha, whether manifested as blissful or wrathful, is never a single subject. Each manifested Buddha has a consort and other companions. Each realm of Buddha is filled with various other beings, such as Dakini. In this way, the *bardo* teaching emphasizes the communal nature of the world of Nirvana, and this communal element can empower immigrants, who often feel alone.

Finally, the teaching of *bardo* manifests border-crossing spirituality by focusing on determination and choice, which is involved at every moment, even the moments after death. If we think of immigrant life, it is very common to find deep feelings of restlessness, anxiety, and powerlessness. Most often, immigrants do not express their feelings and thoughts, and become voiceless. As Homi Bhabha indicates, the power of the dislocated immigrant person lies in the ability to articulate her or his situation, which means living in the third space or an in-between space.[30] Once persons can articulate their situation, they gain more freedom and power by residing in the third space, a space of "in-between."

Bardo is a dangerous and violent place, but also a space for opportunity. The main teaching of *bardo* is that every moment when the soul experiences a tumultuous or a blissful vision can be an opportunity to gain liberation. Once the soul realizes the true nature of all phenomena, the violent place becomes an entrance to liberation and freedom. Sogyal Rinpoche elaborates the nature of *bardo* as borderland by saying that while the nature of *bardo* is violent, there are many opportunities to gain transformation by embracing all kinds of life experience.[31]

Another opportunity for transformation exists in types of marginality, such as cultural, sexual, and social. According to the *bardo* teaching, in a vision, the soul should embrace the other,

30. Bhabha, *Location of Culture*, 28.

31. Rinpoche, *Tibetan Book of Living and Dying*, 89.

who is the Buddha nature manifested as a threatening unfamiliar figure. Similarly, immigrants need to accept the other or otherness encountered in this life, and that is the core of borderland spirituality.

As Gloria Anzaldúa describes in *Borderlands la Frontera: The New Mestiza,* the borderland is a space of violence and danger, but it is also a space for transformation.[32] In realizing the importance of now-ness, celebrating community or friendship, and especially, choosing to embrace the uncomfortable situation as it is, the teaching of *bardo* illuminates borderland spirituality.

32. Anzaldúa, *Borderlands*, 100.

4

A Border-Crossing Dance

Spiritual Direction with the Other

SPIRITUAL DIRECTION IS ONE of our most ancient, yet still vibrant, spiritual practices and ministries. It can easily be called spiritual friendship, companionship, or soul mates, but the main idea is to create a space in which a seeker can find the meaning of life and of lived experience. Almost every religious tradition has developed various types of spiritual direction, through which people experience growth in faith and transformation. Of course, transformation includes the deepening of relationships with the sacred, understanding of self and others, and responding to the signs of time and space. Spiritual direction can happen in various settings, but in this chapter, I will address formal individual spiritual direction, in which the two parties make a covenant and commit a time and space for the seeker.

Using the metaphor of a journey for the spiritual life, seekers experience mysteries or encounter a myriad of moments that need to be explored, and often this process of exploration triggers certain memories, events, and emotions. Frequently, the discourse of spiritual direction emphasizes the ministerial aspect and, consequently, pays attention to possible benefits for seekers, which catalyze as a deepening relationship with God.[1] In other words, the focus is given to the seeker's transformation.

However, if the spiritual director listens to the seeker's journey attentively, is it possible for the mystery that the director witnesses to remain intact? For me, spiritual direction is a dance between a spiritual director and a seeker. The seeker brings the rhythm, to which the spiritual director must be attuned. In this dance, the seeker and the companion, who walks along with the seeker, construct a space together. In the dynamics of spiritual direction, the space, which emerges through the action of border -crossing between the seeker and the spiritual director, includes many possibilities for transformation. In the border-crossing action, through the guidance of the spirit, the spiritual director and the seeker experience *mutual* transformation.

The borderland created in spiritual direction suggests that, in the "in-between space," a seeker freely explores the experience, savoring and examining it, and the seeker finds a possible meaning of life. Yet, at the same time, the borderland invites the spiritual director to gain spiritual knowledge in depth and to experience transformation by crossing the border of her/his own understanding of God and of the world.

In this chapter, I will explore the meaning of spiritual direction as a process of border-crossing, addressing why spiritual direction can be understood as a borderland from the seeker's perspective, as well as from that of the director. Also, I will examine the border-crossing dynamics in terms of today's society. In this way, I will delineate the border-crossing spirituality of attentive listening, the preferential option for the stranger, and hospitality.

SPIRITUAL DIRECTION AS THE BORDERLAND

The borderland signifies the area where the border is located. In the borderland, two or three different cultures encounter and clash. Here, the concept of place can indicate a site or location,

1. Barry, "Spiritual Direction," 31–34.

while space may be movement or process. Focusing on movement rather than fixed a site or a location, the borderland is not a stagnant place, but rather an active space.[2] As a consequence, the borderland space can be characterized as unstable, mobile, and violent. Yet, surprisingly, the borderland is the space where an experience can be accepted as it is, and where new possibilities burgeon. This space, created through the dynamics of encounter between different cultures, changes the landscape of the culture.

Actually, the concept of the borderland does not always appeal as an image of spiritual direction. Very often, spiritual direction is identified with a calm and serene place, such a beautiful retreat or Zen center, where the seeker sits with the spiritual director over a cup of tea. The outlook of spiritual direction could certainly be depicted in this way; however, spiritual direction is a movement or process. I describe spiritual direction as *the internal space* and, more specifically, a borderland space in which a seeker and a director create and explore possible dynamics in the process of, and movements toward, spiritual transformation.

Borderland from a Seeker's Perspective

From the perspective of a seeker, spiritual direction could be understood as the borderland, where ambiguity and uncertainty are fully accepted, and where fragmented ideas are treated as a whole. In this space, fragments of life experiences, which are not yet integrated in one's soul, exist in a state of *dissonance*, which causes intensive emotions such as anxiety, frustration, anger, sadness, etc. In the "in-between" space of spiritual direction, the seekers can look freely into the experience and explore the raw emotions, thoughts, and imagination that are as yet neither processed nor named. This action can be like looking at an object through a kaleidoscope.

2. Creswell, *Place*, 8.

Jacqueline Lewis explains that the borderland requires a sense of safety or holding as a space for transformation and creativity,[3] utilizing the theory of Donald W. Winnicottt. As a child psychologist, Winnicott explains that children in transition need safe objects or assuring actions, such as holding, affirming, and loving.[4] Expanding on this childhood transition into daily adult life, the need for a safe environment can be applied to spiritual direction. Thus, a sense of safety and security is one of the most crucial elements in spiritual direction practice in the borderland, and it attributes to the competency and virtue of spiritual director.

It is not rare to encounter seekers who forcefully try to integrate their life into the ideal, something too elusive to master. The spiritual life, as an organic process, unfolds and perhaps the spiritual task of every seeker is to embrace the resulting absurdity. Therefore, the image of spiritual direction is much more like a borderland where all absurd experiences of life can be held securely.

In contemporary society, one of the dangerous temptations we struggle against is effectiveness or productivity. Even in spiritual matters, seekers hasten to delve into the productive meaning in a very systemic way. However, in spiritual direction, certain experiences or aspects of self can remain entangled, and not integrated. When a seeker understands spiritual direction as a borderland negating integration that forces people to hastily move into a direction, the seeker will feel freedom.

In the safety of the borderland space, a seeker can honestly face reality and oneself. Etty Hillesum, a young Jewish woman who embraced her fragile personality and her challenges during the Nazi regime, and who willingly walked into Auschwitz, claims that honesty is the essential element of being a mystic.[5] In her diary, readers see how boldly she opened up her vulnerable aspects of life to the truth and, by staying in the process honestly, reached the level of seeing the beauty of the creator in the midst of the

3. Lewis, *Power of Stories*, 16.

4. Ibid., 24.

5. Hillesum, *Etty*, 426.

concentration camp and sharing the destiny of all other Jews in her perspective of life.

In the safe space, there exist together three aspects of a seeker: the real, the symbolic, and the imaginary. Psychologist Jacque Lacan argues that human subjectivity is composed of the real, the symbolic, and the imaginary dimensions, employing the concept of the Borromean ring: the three rings are intertwined, but once one dimension of the three is severed, the whole ring is resolved.[6] In Lacan's theory, the real signifies the unknown area or the realm of infinite negation, which signifies what "is not," is unknown, and is a hidden dimension of truth. In the context of spiritual direction, the real can be God, or any mystery of life, which cannot yet be named. Then, the two other dimensions of the imaginary and the symbolic are mediums through which the seeker constructs and comprehends the mystery of life, including the experience of God.

Through the symbolic dimension, the seeker can name and tease out the experience in the context of culture and within the structure of society; through the imaginary dimension, the seeker can project any transforming vision of God and experience liberation from social obligation or norms. In this topography, if the imaginative dimension over-emphasizes, the subject will become narcissistic or arbitrary, while if the symbolic is overly focused, the subject become strict, blindly following social norms or culture. Thus, the role of the spiritual director is to balance in this dynamics of a seeker, holding the person in a safe environment.

The virtue of the seeker is to open up to the process, not being hasty or forcing oneself into the ideal state. The spirit of openness includes the generosity to accept oneself as one is and hold any unfamiliar stories of oneself as sacred in the borderland space of spiritual direction. In the borderland, people who seek spiritual transformation remember the past without resentment or guilt, project into the future in hope and faith, but fundamentally remain in the present. Thus, in the borderland, the time frames of the past, present, and future cross borders freely. However, the

6. Mitchell and Rose, *Feminine Sexuality*, 171.

seeker deepens the understanding self, others, and God by focusing strongly on the current situation, on the present.

Here, focusing on the present means that the past can be interpreted in as many ways as possible, so as to indicate the present and to project into the future; and the future can be imagined freely from the perspective of the present and the past. In the safety of the borderland, the virtue of courage to be honest and to open to the unknown path can be enhanced through the process of learning how to trust in God and to comprehend self.

Borderland from Director's Perspective

No doubt, spiritual direction is a covenant, intentionally given to the seeker. Very often, the discourses of spiritual direction emphasize the role of the spiritual director, who supposedly exists to help the seeker. In this case, the role of the spiritual director is, through holy listening, to reveal to seekers the presence of God.[7] In relation to this approach, one of the most well-known images of spiritual director is a midwife, as coined by Margaret Geunther,[8] which is much more like a good teacher. This image implies that the spiritual directee is the recipient of the spiritual direction. In this way, most discourses of spiritual direction do not go further regarding the dynamics between the spiritual director and the seeker, from how a spiritual director can serve the seeker. Most dialogue is about how the spiritual director keeps boundaries so that the integrity remains intact.

Focusing on the dynamics between the spiritual director and the seeker, spiritual direction can be understood as a borderland in that the spiritual director leaves his/her own comfort zone by *listening* to, or engaging with, the new and unexpected rhythms of the spirits. This process can be called a borderland, which negates any stable home or state of mind. As Mexican feminist Gloria

7. Jones, *Exploring Spiritual Direction*, 4.

8. Guenther, *Holy Listening*, 82.

Anzaldúa suggests, there is no longer such a home which continues the journey in the faith, and the process itself becomes home.[9]

As a spiritual director, one of the distinct calls of the borderland of spiritual direction is to encounter strangers or foreigners and provide them with hospitality. Any seeker who comes to the director is a stranger. When a spiritual director meets a seeker, the director might feel comfortable when the seeker belongs to the same religious tradition or ethnic group. However, sooner or later, the spiritual director will notice differences between the seeker and him/herself. For example, as a Korean immigrant, when I meet a Korean seeker, I initially feel comfortable and assume the seeker has the same cultural values as mine. However, often, it proves to be untrue.

Because culture is not a static block of data, but rather a dynamic process of living and ever-changing patterns of life, differing from context to context in terms of life times and circumstances,[10] it is impossible to meet anyone who has the same value of culture. Almost every individual has various subcultures such as class, gender, education, sexual orientation, political view, and generation, and thus each person carries multiple identities.

Then, it would be fair to say that a spiritual director always encounters a stranger and through the engagement with the stranger, a borderland space emerges. What happens to the spiritual director through the encounter with the stranger? In Greek, the term "brutish," literally meaning beast-like, indicates a person who does not use the faculty of reason and politically implies non-Greek citizens who are strangers or foreigners. Perhaps in the fairy tale of the *Beauty and the Beast*, the moment that the female character Belle encounters the beast captures the encounter between a spiritual director and a seeker. In this world of the fairy tale, the essential quality of a beast is its *otherness*, which can be summarized as a representation of the unknown and shadowy aspects of human nature.[11]

9. Anzaldúa, "Preface," 3.

10. Houtepen, "Intercultural Theology," 29.

11. Hallett and Karasek, *Folk and Fairy Tales*, 172.

Then, what are the feelings and emotions that emerge through encountering the stranger? Perhaps what arises is a sense of discomfort and, more deeply, a sense of fear, fear of the unknown in particular. Fear often can be expressed as a sign of the scary appearance of a non-human being or the beast, in the case of the fairy tale.[12] In fact, in many fairy tales, the encounter of a beast leads the hero or heroine to a different level of life or self-understanding.

In the borderland space, the spiritual director might feel a fear of the unknown as a consequence of border-crossing, and this fear can invite the director into her/his own spiritual growth. Actually, the fear of the unknown has a symbolic meaning. Fear or discomfort as an action of facing a stranger is called "uncanny strangeness" (Heimlich/Unheimlich), a term emphasized by Freud. The word *Unheimlich*, paradoxically, is already close to its opposite meaning, because the word *Heimlich* means "friendly comfortable," yet, at the same time, also means "concealed, kept from sight, or behind someone's back."[13]

Then, since the expression "uncanny strangeness" insinuates a psychological meaning of the unknown self that one carries, it is comfortable but at the same time scary. Furthermore, following Freud's notion of uncanny strangeness, feminist psychologist Julia Kristeva insists, "the stranger is neither race nor a nation . . . Uncanny, foreignness is within us: we are our own foreigners."[14] In other words, the discomfort in encountering newness and fear caused by the foreign could be a part of the director's unknown self.

Understanding the feeling of "uncanny strangeness," which pops up in one's mind when facing the "other," can be an opportunity to see a true and hidden-self. A well-known short story, "The Tiger's Bride," by Angela Carter, shows the internal dimension of beastliness that we all carry. In this story, a girl is forced to stay with a tiger due to her father's gambling loss. One day, the tiger, representing the other or foreignness, asks her to show her naked

12. Park, "Cross-Cultural Spiritual Direction," 29.

13. Kristeva, *Strangers to Ourselves*, 182.

14. Ibid., 181.

body in exchange for her release. In embarrassment, shame, and fear, she says, "I was unaccustomed to nakedness. I was so unused to *my own skin* that to take off all my clothes involved a kind flying . . . "[15] (emphasis mine). This short story finishes with these impressive lines:

> And each stroke of his tongue ripped off skin after successive skin, all the skins of a life in the world, and left behind a nascent patina of shining hairs. My earrings turned back to water and trickled down my shoulders: I shrugged the drops off my beautiful fur.[16]

After overcoming the fear caused by her unfamiliarity, she finds her own beast-likeness or *otherness*, which is an aspect of her unknown self.

Defining the shadow as an unknown part of self, the internal shadow is the flip side of the external shadow. The external shadow manifests the social condition that dictates or forces one into a certain pattern of action and reaction. For example, once a spiritual director has been educated that poverty is a consequence of idleness, the spiritual director's action or reaction to the poor is judgmental rather than compassionate. Through an encounter with the stranger struggling over issues of poverty in the midst of strenuous work, the spiritual director can expand the horizon of her/his understanding of poverty.

Through the action of border-crossing, the spiritual director grows one's own self-knowledge, including an embrace of one's shadow or unknown self, and for this process, the spiritual director needs to be equipped with a spirit of hospitality. Hospitality is a recurring theme throughout the history of Christianity, as well as in the Bible. In the Hebrew Scripture, hospitality is described as a way to meet and entertain God. In Genesis 18, three strangers visit Abraham and his response to the strangers shows an example of hospitality. Once he sees the strangers, Abraham provides hospitality with a good dinner and receives blessings from them.

15. Carter, "Tiger's Bride," 66.

16. Ibid., 66.

Interestingly enough, Abraham does not even know who they are or whether they are friends or enemies. In a sense, thus, hospitality is a risky action of trusting and opening oneself to the other.

Furthermore, the spirituality of hospitality has been emphasized as a virtue of the desert fathers and mothers, who provided wisdom and shelter to people who came to visit the spiritual masters in the desert. Thomas Merton argues that the tradition of spiritual direction emerged from the Desert.[17] When Christianity was accepted by the Roman Empire in 313 CE, many Christians left the empire and sought deeper wisdom in the desert. According to Peter Brown, there were socio-political reasons why many people went to the desert. Because of a high taxation policy, many peasants ran away to the wilderness and often consulted the wisdom of the masters, who were shrewd about political tactics for fighting against the Roman Empire; the desert became a space for hospitality.[18] The desert is not far from the city, but distant enough from it—or at least on the margins of the empire—that people could explore a new vision of spiritual and political life. Thus, the desert is a borderland in which, for the purposes of survival, the most important virtue is to provide hospitality with others.

Literally and figuratively, the desert is a space for seeking wisdom in the midst of danger from beasts and of hunger and thirst. Spiritual masters, called Desert Father or Desert Mother, lived in the desert where seekers—including novices in desert monastic life—visited the masters for wisdom. Perhaps beginners, who are determined to live in the desert, need a guide who has certain knowledge in order to survive in the harsh environment as well as to flourish in spiritual growth. One of the most dangerous things to deal with in the desert is one's inner demon, which can be the narcissistic ego, expressed as craving or greed, vainglory, hatred, anger, sexual desire, or fear. Desert Fathers' sayings show how the masters led seekers in a kind, gentle, and—more importantly—practical way, based on their own experiences. In the

17. Innes, "Wisdom from the Desert."

18. Brown, *Body and Society*, 132.

desert tradition of spiritual direction, the position of the director is of great importance.

However, nowadays in spiritual direction, there are new movements focused on the dynamics between the spiritual director and the seeker. For example, all acting spiritual directors belong to a peer supervision group or have a supervisor. This could be interpreted as an overly careful action by the director, but the supervision provides a space where the spiritual director can look into the experience of border-crossing. In other words, supervision aims to help the spiritual director examine and explore a certain border-crossing action with a certain directee.

The understanding of hospitality can be expanded even further. The virtue of hospitality can be practiced on the level of switching the roles of host and guest. According to Jacque Derrida, hospitality happens in the space "originally belonging to neither host nor guest, but to the gesture by which one of them welcomes the other."[19] In other words, hospitality is an interaction and a dynamic between a seeker and a spiritual director, a consequence of which is that the spiritual director takes the role of a guest or stranger and the seeker becomes a host who is charge and becomes the leader. In this logic, spiritual direction is an action of hospitality in which the spiritual director voluntarily takes the place of stranger, a person in a vulnerable position.

In Luke's Gospel, the story of Emmaus (Luke 24:13–32) shows the spirituality of radical hospitality. On the way to Jerusalem, two disciples who are disappointed at Jesus' death encounter a stranger. They open their hearts and talk about their sadness and frustration resulting from the death of Jesus, not knowing about or believing in the resurrection of Jesus. At dusk, these two disciples invite the stranger to come to their place. In this story, oddly enough, the stranger breaks the bread—which is usually the role of the host—then offers the meal blessings and gives the bread to the host. It is almost like an unexpected stranger coming to a family's Thanksgiving dinner and carving the turkey. Of course, this line about the stranger breaking the bread shows the liturgical formula

19. Derrida, *Of Hospitality*, 67.

of the Eucharist. As readers of the Bible, we know that the stranger is the risen Jesus, and so the story does not feel weird to us. However, the story strongly shows an example of radical hospitality in that the guest becomes the host and the host becomes a guest.

This radical hospitality seems to result in the disciples having a perspective of a life event: what happened to their life and commitment as disciples. They remember how they were happy and touched when the stranger was with them. Then finally, they come back to the community of disciples. This story could be interpreted as a spirituality of radical spirituality in that the disciples experience an expansion of self-understanding as followers of Jesus Christ.

This story invites the spiritual director to give up all assumptions in spiritual direction, to situate oneself into a more vulnerable spot, and to surrender to the process. In other words, the spiritual director must embrace a deep feeling of discomfort and fear, keeping only an attentive love. Here, the attentive love emphasizes losing control, opening to the process, and acknowledging life is not on his or her ground.[20] Thus, as a practice of hospitality, the spiritual director is then ready for the attentive love in which he/she is willing to adjust to the agenda brought in the encounter and to let go of previous standards of morality, culture, and faith.

THE BORDERLAND TODAY

Today's life can be characterized as border-crossing. On the one hand, in this globalized world, which would be represented as immigration and experiences of dislocation, border-crossings—in terms of culture, territory, and religion—occur easily. Multiculturalism is, consequently, apparent. In any urban city, it is common to see an Islamic center across the street from a Christian church or a Buddhist temple. It is easy to meet people from different denominations in the Christian tradition, as well as from other religions. Further, there is great possibility of encountering a seeker from

20. Ruddick, *Maternal Thinking*, 183.

another culture or religion, or both. Through this border-crossing action, a new culture or hybrid spirituality emerges.

Significantly, the internalized border-crossing aspect appears as the "not religious, but spiritual" phenomena, referred to by the acronym NRBS. A notable and growing number of Americans do not identify themselves as members of any religion. According to a 2013 Pew Report, 20 percent of Americans—a whopping one-fifth of the adult population—describe themselves as religiously unaffiliated. That number is up from 15 percent just five years ago, and the percentage is higher for those younger—up to 72 percent for Generation Y, those born after 1980. As such, the majority of spiritual seekers and spiritual directors are therefore "not religious, but spiritual."

Furthermore, it is not rare to meet one who is different from the spiritual director in terms of gender, social class, sexual orientation, age, race, and ethnicity, even within the same religious tradition. Thus, spiritual direction today shows more severely the border-crossing dynamics between a director and a seeker.

The Three Dynamics of Border-Crossing

Recent discourse on spiritual direction has moved the focus to seekers who are from different cultures, a movement which reflects our cross-cultural reality. In intercultural discourse, one of the main concerns is the religious dimension, emphasizing where and when the border of syncretism transgressed.[21] However, because of recent mass movements of people from the South to the North, as well as economic and social issues such as human trafficking and the global financial crisis,[22] the focus has changed into the spiritual dimension of border-crossing, along with spiritual transformation and interconnectedness.

There are three ways to understand border-crossing in multicultural and interfaith contexts. First is when a seeker comes to a

21. Friedli, "Postscript," 129.

22. Ibid., 132.

spiritual director who does not represent the same faith tradition. Who would be willing to come to a spiritual director who is unfamiliar with his or her own culture and religion? It could be someone who wants to examine new perspectives of life. When a seeker wants to explore deeper meanings without the attachment of his/her religious tradition, the seeker often looks for a different reference. As such, in regard to his/her spiritual journey, for a certain time period, the seeker could seek a spiritual director from other traditions. For example, a seeker who has some knowledge or a certain attraction to a particular spiritual tradition could come to a spiritual director from that tradition. The seeker could have a desire to deepen and widen an understanding of self, others, and God through crossing the border of spiritual traditions. Or, the case may be that the seeker cannot find a spiritual director from his/her own spiritual tradition because of the person's location or situation.

In the book, *Spiritual Guidance across Religions*, the editor explicitly states that in our current society, which is multicultural and multi-religious, it is not easy to find spiritual directors in their home spiritual tradition.[23] For example, for an African woman from a certain tradition or for a Zoroastrian from India, it is very difficult to find spiritual directors from those same traditions. Or in the case of certain minority groups, the pool of directors is so narrow that the choice is highly limited in terms of subcategories, such as a liberal politics, class, gender, or education.

In border-crossing spiritual direction, the spiritual director should listen to the seeker's desire and help the seeker articulate it. New concepts or terms from a different spiritual tradition can illuminate the meaning of life. Here, the task of the spiritual director is to adjust to the seeker through attentive listening, without any given assumptions. However, at the same time, the seeker might feel frustrated from terminology or vocabulary that is unfamiliar. The seeker should try to feel comfortable asking for clarity with any concept, while the spiritual director should openly listen to the seeker and not try to hear from only her/his own framework.

23. Mabry, "Introduction," ix–x.

Another example of border-crossing dynamics could emerge from the group of "not religious, but spiritual." Someone who claims no specific religious tradition and practices certain prayers or meditation would like to meet a spiritual director. These people are serious about their spiritual paths, but they never limit their search to a single tradition. They are open to wisdom, beliefs, and practices of many different spiritual, philosophical, and humanist traditions. They often carry multiple identities; for them, identity is fluid. In this case, the seeker does not have any specific references, or else uses the specific terms or practices of the director. For example, college students who come to spiritual direction might not attend church services, but they still want to grow in their spirituality. They pray, but it is hard to define what kind of prayer they practice. For those seekers, the spiritual director should listen attentively, focusing on their story, feelings, and thought, neither interpreting nor providing a frame to interpret it.

One of the main characteristics of the NRBS is flexibility in learning new concepts. As an attentive listener who focuses on the seeker's experience without specific frameworks, after fully listening to the seeker, the spiritual director can provide useful references. For example, when a seeker struggles with the experience of success and fame, the spiritual director could introduce the Tao Te Ching and biblical passages together. Especially, younger generation of the NRBS likely have no religious background or education, and are less informed.[24] It is quite different from the NRBS of Gen X and baby boomers who claim no religious affiliation.

For them, the spiritual director needs to hold the experience consistently because the seeker could be unfocused, lacking consistency, and continuously looking for new concepts. Also, this kind of seeker has a tendency to be idealistic in terms of spiritual growth and transformation. For this, the spiritual director should help the seeker be grounded in the here and now, and remind her/him that ups and downs in the spiritual journey are normal.[25] The seeker can be challenged by the director through an invitation into

24. Ibid., ix–xi.

25. Mabry, "Spiritual Guidance," 381.

the deep, which can be characterized by staying here, now, in the midst of darkness, even while lacking clarity and direction.

On the contrary, when the seeker brings in a new concept unfamiliar to the director, the director should have the inner freedom to ask about it. In this way, the spiritual director can be challenged. The director's assumption-free questions can help the seeker dig into the deeper meaning of the experience. In this dialogue, the director can learn how the seeker uses the terms or concepts and interpret the seeker's life experience through those concepts. At the same time, the director can deepen and widen one's own spirituality.

The last category is the seeker who claims multiple religious belonging. These people look similar to the NRBS in that they bring the teachings or wisdom of various traditions and religions, but they are distinct in that they claim to inherit or own various spiritual traditions and religions. According to Catherine Cornille, the term "multiple religious belonging" was coined in the twenty-first century and is delineated into two types: involuntary and based on social and cultural contexts; and deliberate and based on personal need or choice.[26]

For those who are Asians or Asian Americans, Confucianism, Buddhism, and Taoism operate simultaneously. Among those seekers, it is hard to tease out specific aspects because these three different elements are integrated in their culture and daily life. For example, the Chinese Christian author John Wu, who is the author of *Beyond East and West,* articulates his spiritual journey to God, using Asian religious expressions. In his book, every thread of Christian spirituality is woven with the thread of Asian spirituality. Also, many Asian biblical scholars, such as Sungai Ha, have tried to interpret the Bible from a Daoist perspective.[27]

In other cases, people practice double religions or spirituality due to marriage. For example, a Buddhist who marries a Christian carries two very different religions in one, a task which is sometimes incredibly tough. While differences in religions can be well

26. Cornille, "Multiple Religious Belonging," 325.

27. Ha, "Reading of the Divine Speech."

negotiated, most often they cause serious conflicts between the couple, as well as with other family members.

Furthermore, there are often cases of voluntary hybrid religious practices. Union Seminary professor Paul Knitter, in *Without Buddha I Could Not Be a Christian*, explains his spiritual journey this way:

> I can truly call myself what I think I've been over these past decades: a Buddhist Christian. . . . This 'double belonging' has enriched his life and faith in profound and meaningful ways.[28]

For those people, the other practice affirms and deepens their original faith. In spiritual direction, the spiritual director could meet the seeker at various stages of the journey: when the seeker tries to enter the other religion, or integrate the two religions, or leaving the original religion. In any case, the role of the spiritual director is to listen attentively and respect the new journey of the seeker.

BORDER-CROSSING SPIRITUALITY

Naming the presence is the always the gateway to pursuing the truth. In the context of spiritual direction, naming the presence, I believe, emphasizes being "now and here" with the seeker, who might easily be multi-ethnic, inter-faith, and multi-vocal. Putting aside one's own spiritual concerns, the spiritual director is then invited to a dance with a stranger. In the context of spiritual direction as border crossing and in contemporary society in particular, how can borderland spirituality be summarized?

First, border-crossing spirituality is attentive listening. Listening is an action of contemplative love. It implies that the listener pays attention to the speaker in terms of speech, body gesture, and silence. In this way, the listener does not hold any judgments based on one's own cultural, spiritual, and social assumptions. The listener should be open to the deeper level of self-knowledge. Through

28. Knitter, *Without Buddha*, 237.

the encounter, the listener should be challenged or invited into the realm of the unknown. All kinds of fear, as described above, which are often projected onto the seeker, are actually the shadows of the spiritual director.

Attentive listening is, according to Sara Ruddick, expressed as maternal thinking, which can be characterized as follows: adjusting to the situation, losing control over the situation, and opening to the process.[29] Ruddick describes that the maternal way of thinking and of being creates peace. In this way, the mother's attentive love signifies the way that one is willing to adjust to the need of others. The more one adjusts oneself to the other and the needs of the other, the more one becomes open to the process. Also, I believe that the maternal way of thinking lies in the attitude of letting go of control and letting go of the situation. For example, a mother should let her child go when the child grows. This attitude, when applied to spiritual direction, will give the spiritual director a great deal of freedom.

The second element of border-crossing spirituality can be addressed as a preferential option for the stranger. In daily life, we are called to meet the stranger, who can be in the form of a foreigner or a neighbor. However, these strangers bring a new dimension of life and, very often, the unknown or unfamiliar part of what is brought is a message from God.[30] This unfamiliarity is an invitation to extend one's own concept of self, the other, and God.

In the context of spiritual direction, the spiritual director's moral obligation should be a preferential option for the stranger. The stranger can be *the other,* in terms of ethnicity, religion, spirituality, gender, sexual orientation, class, etc. The more one embraces the stranger, the more the one embraces oneself. The action of the option for the stranger is deeply related to the spirituality of hospitality.

Hospitality is the central spirituality of the borderland in spiritual direction. Hospitality is the virtue of being vulnerable and open to the stranger. The spiritual writer Henri Nouwen, in

29. Ruddick, *Maternal Thinking*, 131.

30. Palmer, *Company of Strangers*, 68.

Reaching Out: The Three Moments of Spiritual Life, explains that in terms of the relationship between a guest and a host, hospitality lies on the host's receptivity to what the guest brings.[31] Of course, this receptivity requires risking safety and befriending fear.

Nevertheless, this receptivity changes the dynamics of spiritual direction into a dance of mutual transformation. As Diarmuid O'Murchu says, when the seeker's story unfolds, the director's life unfolds.[32] In this dance, both transcend the designated roles, in which the spiritual director guides the seeker, and each serves the other.[33] In other words, the host becomes the guest, and the guest becomes the host.

This dance requires the seeker to be open and honest in the process. By being honest in the dynamic, the seeker challenges the director and this challenge will be a gift for the director, as long as it is embraced sincerely and openly. The director needs to hold safely onto the seeker, surrendering to the story of the seeker, and giving up one's own assumptions, judgment, and framework. In this radical hospitality, in which the host becomes the guest and the guest becomes the host, these two mutually experience transformation.

31. Nouwen, *Reaching Out*, 67.

32. O'Murchu, "New Paradigms in Spiritual Direction" (Audio recording).

33. Hay, *Hospitality*, 30.

Conclusion

IN TODAY'S WORLD, MANY people experience border-crossings within the mechanisms of global capitalism, dynamics of multiculturalism, and abundance of social media. Upon crossing one's border and entering into the unknown, people experience social, cultural, and even economic change. As such, it is necessary to seek the meaning of such experiences. Border-crossings have been considered, in many spiritual traditions, as processes of transformation and empowerment.

Observing the spiritual wisdom that is embedded in sacred texts such as the Christian Bible, the Gospel in particular, border-crossing spirituality stresses the importance of opening up to and grasping new opportunities —for survival, as well as for spiritual transformation. In the harsh lives of the marginalized, including new immigrants from other cultures, survival can be the most crucial dimension of the lived experience. Once one gains a sense of survival, the person ideally can walk into spiritual transformation by gaining a sense of subjectivity and regaining social membership. For those border-crossing people, survival is never less important than spiritual matters.

The Tibetan Book of the Dead, a sacred text from the Tibetan Buddhist tradition, indicates a border-crossing spirituality that pays special attention the importance of *now and here* in one's life. All detailed teachings culminate at the point that all sentient beings should face life as it is, without fear, resentment, or disappointment. As such, the text about death and the journey between after death and rebirth, paradoxically talks about life. Even potential dangerous moments of the in-between, called *bardo* according to the Tibetan text, can be meaningful for Enlightenment.

Border-crossing spirituality can be obtained from ritual studies, and in particular, from the shamanic rituals of Jeju Island, located between South Korea and Japan. Ritual creates an in-between space, and the case study of Jeju Island shows characteristics of the borderland. Although Jeju is a territory of South Korea, the island has had a long history of oppression and exploitation by the dwellers of the Korean peninsula, and, in 1948, many innocent Jeju islanders were killed by the US military government. This hidden tragedy of the island has been expressed through the shaman rituals, and the ritual space has become a force to articulate, reveal, and resist oppressive power, as well as to express the desire to heal wounds and create a new identity for Jeju.

In contrast to its quietly isolated history, Jeju Island has become a borderland where diverse cultures encounter each other, due to immigration from the Korean peninsula and the development of international commerce and tourism. As a consequence, Jeju Island manifests cultural elements of a borderland in that traditional lifestyles and westernized styles, and native islanders and immigrants co-exist, but are not fully integrated. However, the island is showing a transforming aspect of a borderland in the midst of the island's struggle to proclaim itself as the *peace island*, including years of resistance against the construction of a navy base on the island. As a political borderland, Jeju Island offers a border-crossing spirituality which constructs a new hybrid identity and fights against oppressive powers, and which tries to recover their traumatic history, in congruence with a shamanic ritual which is an ancient spiritual practice.

Furthermore, one of the apparent areas of border-crossing spirituality can be revealed in the practice of spiritual direction, which has been developed in many spiritual and religious traditions. Traditionally, the relationship between a seeker and a spiritual director was one in which the director had authority over the seeker. Authority was given with the understanding that the spiritual director had apt knowledge and experience in spiritual matters. Often in the discourse of spiritual direction, emphasis was given to the director as to how to keep boundaries.

Recently, the spiritual direction relationship has been rearticulated as mutual, and through such a mutual relationship, the spiritual director and the seeker can both experience transformation. The space created in spiritual direction can be a borderland where the two parties are seriously engaged, for the sake of the seeker. Thus, the role of the spiritual director is to listen attentively and, in so doing, help the seeker understand the experience of life and experience spiritual transformation. The requirement of the seeker is to trust and be open to the process, paying attention to any inner movements regarding the concern that the seeker brings to the space of spiritual direction.

In the relationship of spiritual direction, the party who must embrace otherness is the spiritual director. There is not a single person who carries the same idea or experiences as the spiritual director. Even when a spiritual director meets a seeker from the same faith tradition or ethnic group, the spiritual director must understand that the seeker is different. Thus, the ministry of spiritual direction is, by nature, supposed to embrace the other. The other can be categorized as gender, religious tradition or practice, class, ethnicity, and race, plus many more different subcategories.

One of the most common reactions to the other is fear and discomfort, but that fear can be understood as the fear in facing one's own shadow or unknown aspect. Thus, when a spiritual director meets a seeker who is different, if the seeker causes the spiritual director a great sense of fear, the seeker can be called the other who challenges the spiritual director to further deepen one's self-knowledge. In the process of mutual transformation, the most necessary virtue is hospitality.

In today's multicultural and interreligious culture, which involves multiple dimensions of border-crossings, border-crossing spirituality signifies the importance of being in-between, articulating the experience of the borderland as source for wisdom of transformation.

Bibliography

Alonso, Pablo. *The Woman Who Changed Jesus: Crossing Boundaries in MK 7,24–30*. Leuven, Belgium: Peeters, 2011.

Anzaldúa, Gloria. *Borderlands la Frontera: Mew Mestiza*. 3rd ed. San Francisco: Aunt Lute, 2007.

———. Preface to *This Bridge We Call Home: Radical Visions for Transformation*, edited by Gloria Anzaldúa and AnaLousie Keating, 3. New York: Routledge, 2002

Barry, William A. "What Is Spiritual Direction? A Retrospective Reflection." *Presence* 21 (2015) 31–34.

Bell, Catherine. *Ritual Theory, Ritual Practice*. Oxford: Oxford University Press, 1992.

Berling, Judith A. *Understanding Other Religious Worlds: A Guide for Interreligious Education*. Maryknoll: Orbis, 2004.

Bhabha, Homi. *The Location of Culture*. New York: Routledge, 1996.

Brock, Rita Nakashima. *Journeys by Heart: A Christology of Erotic Power*. New York: Crossroad, 1988.

Brown, Peter. *The Body and Society: Men, Women, and Sexual Renunciation in Early Christianity*. New York: Columbia University Press, 1988.

Buber, Martin. *I and Thou*. New York: Touchstone, 1996.

Carter, Angela. "The Tiger's Bride." In *The Bloody Chamber*, 51–67. New York: Penguin, 1981.

Cheon, Kyoungsu, et al. *Reinterpretation of Jeju History*. Jeju Studies Series 8. Jeju: Jeju Development Institute, 2013.

Cho, Sung Hyun. "Toward a Model of Pastoral Preaching in Jeju Island Churches of Korea with Particular Reference to their Cultural Context." DMin diss., San Francisco Theological Seminary, 2008.

Cornille, Catherine. "Multiple Religious Belonging." In *Understanding Interreligious Relations*, edited by David Cheetham et al., 324–40. Oxford: Oxford University Press, 2013.

Coward, Harold. "Jung's Commentary on *The Tibetan Book of the Dead*." In *Self and Liberation: Jung-Buddhism Dialogue*, edited by Daniel J. Meckel and Robert L. Moore, 261–74. New York: Paulist, 1992.

Creswell, Tim. *Place: A Short Introduction*. Oxford: Blackwell, 2004.

Cuevas, Bryan J. *The Hidden History of the Tibetan Book of the Dead*. New York: Oxford University Press, 2003.

Derrida, Jacques. *Of Hospitality: Anne Dufourmantelle Invites Jacques Derrida to Respond*. Stanford: Stanford University Press, 2000.

Dewey, Joanna. "The Gospel of Mark." In *Searching the Scriptures, Volume 2: A Feminist Commentary*, edited by Elisabeth Shússler Fiorenza, 470–509. New York: Crossroad, 1994.

Donahue, John R., and Daniel J. Harrington. *The Gospel of Mark*. Sacra Pagina Series 2. Collegeville, PA: Liturgical, 2002.

Douglas, Mary. *Purity and Danger: An Analysis of Concepts of Pollution and Taboo*. London: Routledge & Kegan Paul, 1966.

Elizondo, Virgilio. *The Future is Mestizo: Life Where Cultures Meet*. Boulder, CO: University of Colorado Press, 2000.

Fremantle, Francesca. "The Tibetan Book of the Dead for the Living." *The Middle Way* 80 (2005) 171–78.

Fremantle, Francesca, and Chögyam Trungpa, trans. *The Tibetan Book of the Dead*. New York: Shambala, 2000.

Friedli, Richard. "Postscript: Variations on 'Intercultural' Retrospectives and Prospectives." In *Intercultural Perceptions and Prospects of World Christianity*, edited by Richard Friedli et al., 127–34. New York: Peter Lang, 2010.

Guenther, Margaret. *Holy Listening: The Art of Spiritual Direction*. Boston: Cowley, 1992.

Ha, Sungai. "A Reading of the Divine Speech in Job in Light of the Zhuangzi: From an Asian Feminist Perspective." PhD diss., Graduate Theological Union, 2013.

Hallett, Martin, and Barbara Karasek, eds. *Folk and Fairy Tales: An Introductory Anthology*. 3rd ed. Peterborough, ON: Broadview, 2002.

Hay, Leslie A. *Hospitality: The Art of Spiritual Direction*. New York: Morehouse, 2006.

Hillesum, Etty. *Etty: The Letters and Dairies of Etty Hillesum, 1941–1943*. Grand Rapids, MI: Eerdmans, 2002.

Hirsch, Eric. "Landscape: Between Place and Space." In *The Anthropology of Landscape: Perspectives on Place and Space*, edited by Eric Hirsch and Michael O'Hanlon, 63–77. Oxford: Clarendon, 1995.

Houtepen, Anton. "Intercultural Theology: A Postmodern Ecumenical Mission." In *Towards an Intercultural Theology*, edited by Martha Frederiks et al., 20–40. Bangalore, India: Centre for Contemporary Christianity, 2010.

Huntington, Samuel. *The Clash of Civilizations and the Remaking of the Social Order*. New York: Touchstone, 1996.

Hur, Namlin. "Jeju's Historical Topos: Periphery and Frontier." *Tamra Culture* 31 (2007) 27.

Hyon, Yong-Joon, *Jeju Musok Yonku*. Seoul: Chipmuntang, 1986.

Innes, D. Keith. "Wisdom from the Desert—The Desert Fathers and Mothers." http://www.ringmerchurch.org.uk/keith2/wisdes.html.

Jones, Alan. *Exploring Spiritual Direction*. Boston: Cowley, 1999.

Ju, Kanghyun. *A Journey on Jeju Island*. Seoul: Woongjin, 2011.

Kim, Elaine H. "Poised on the In-between: A Korean American's Reflections on Theresa Hak Kyoung Cha's Dictée." In *Writing Self, Writing Nation: A Collection of Essays on Dictée by Theresa Hak Kyoung Cha*, edited by Elaine H. Kim et al., 3–34. Berkeley, CA: Third Woman, 1994.

Kim, Jeongsook. *Goddess: Jeju Island, Myth, and Women*. Jeju: Kag, 2006.

Kinukawa, Hisako. *Women and Jesus in Mark: A Japanese Feminist Perspective*. New York: Orbis, 1994.

Kittel, Gerhard, et al., eds. *Theological Dictionary of the New Testament*. Translated by Geoffrey W. Bromily. 9 vols. Grand Rapids, MI: Eerdmans, 1964.

Kleinman, Arthur. "Concepts and a Model for the Comparison of Medical Systems." In *Concepts of Health, Illness and Disease: A Comparative Perspective*, edited by Caroline Currer and Meg Stacey, 29–47. New York: Berg, 1986.

Knitter, Paul F. *Without Buddha, I Could Not Be a Christian*. Croydon, UK: Oneworld, 2013.

Ko, Seongjoon, et al. *East Asia and Jeju, the Island of Peace*. Jeju: Jeju National University Press, 2004.

Kristeva, Julia. *Strangers to Ourselves*. New York: Columbia University Press, 1991.

Lama Lodru. *Bardo Teachings: The Way of Death and Rebirth*. San Francisco: KDK, 1982.

Lee, Janet. "Menarche and the (Hetero)Sexualization of the Female Body." In *The Politics of Women's Bodies: Sexuality, Appearance, and Behavior*, edited by Rose Weitz. London: Oxford University Press, 2003.

Lewis, Jacqueline J. *The Power of Stories: A Guide for Leading Multi-Racial and Multi-Cultural Congregations*. Nashville, TN: Abingdon, 2008.

Mabry, John R. Introduction to *Spiritual Guidance across Religions: A Sourcebook for Spiritual Directors and Other Professionals Providing Counsel to People of Differing Faith Traditions*, edited by John R. Mabry, ix–xi. Woodstock, VT: Skylight Paths, 2014

———. "Spiritual Guidance for Spiritual Eclectics." In *Spiritual Guidance Across Religions: A Sourcebook for Spiritual Directors and Other Professionals Providing Counsel to People of Differing Faith Tradition*, edited by John R. Mabry, 376–84. Woodstock, VT: Skylight Paths, 2014.

Malbon, Elizabeth S. "Fallible Followers." *Semeia* 28 (1983) 29–48.

Mann, Christopher S. *Mark: A New Translation with Introduction and Commentary*. Anchor Bible 27. New York: Doubleday, 1986.

Marcus, Joel. *Mark 1–8: A New Translation with Introduction and Commentary*. Anchor Yale Bible 27. New Haven, VT: Yale University Press, 2008.

Marshall, Christopher D. *Faith as a Theme in Mark's Narrative*. Society for New Testament Studies Monograph Series 64. Cambridge: Cambridge University Press, 1989.

Miller, Susan. *Women in Mark's Gospel*. Journal for the Study of the New Testament Supplement Series 259. New York: T. & T. Clark International, 2004.

Mitchell, Juliet, and Jacqueline Rose, eds. *Feminine Sexuality: Jacques Lacan and the école freudienee*. New York: Norton, 1982.

Mullin, Glenn H. *Death and Dying: The Tibetan Tradition*. London: Arkana, 1986.

———. *The Tibetan Book of the Dead*. Illustrated edition. New Delhi, India: Lustre, 2009.

Neumaier-Dargyay, Eva K. "Many Lives—Many Deaths: The Basic Assumptions." In *Life After Death in World Religions*, edited by Harold G. Coward, 87–104. New York: Orbis, 1997.

Nowen, Henri. *Reaching Out: The Three Moments of the Spiritual Life*. New York: Doubleday, 1975.

O'Murchu, Diarmuid. "New Paradigms in Spiritual Direction: Jesus of the People." Wilsonville, OR: Spiritual Directors International Conference, 2002. Audio cassette.

Palmer, Parker, *The Company of Strangers: Christians and the Renewal of America's Public Life*. New York: Crossroad, 1983.

Park, Chansik. *The Truth of 4.3*. Jeju Island: Jeju April 3 Peace Foundation, 2010.

Park, Idong. *Sasam, Our Endless Wounds*. Jeju: Monthly Tourism Jeju, 1990.

Park, Jung Eun Sophia. *A Hermeneutic on Dislocation as Experience: Creating a Borderland, Constructing a Hybrid Identity*. New York: Peter Lang, 2008.

———. "Toward Cross-Cultural Spiritual Direction: When Feeling Is Caught in a Pattern." *Presence: An International Journal of Spiritual Direction* 19 (2013) 27–32

Pilch, John J. *Healing in the New Testament: Insights from the Medical and Mediterranean Anthropology*. Minneapolis, MN: Fortress, 2000.

Prado, Fabricio. "The Fringes of Empire: Recent Scholarship on Colonial Frontiers and Borderlands in Latin America." *History Compass* 10 (2012) 318–33.

Rinpoche, Sogyal. *The Tibetan Book of Living and Dying*. Rev. ed. New York: HarperCollins, 2002.

Rosenblatt, Marie-Eloise. "Gender, Ethnicity, and Legal Considerations in the Hemorrhaging Woman's Story Mark 5:25–34." In *Transformative Encounters: Jesus and Women Re-Viewed*, edited by Ingrid Rosa Kitzberger, 137–61. Leiden: Brill, 2000.

Ruddick, Sara. *Maternal Thinking: Toward a Politics of Peace*. Boston: Beacon, 1995.

Smith, Huston. Introduction to *The Tibetan Book of the Dead*, translated by Robert A. F. Thurman, viii–xv. New York: Quality Paper Book Club, 1994.

Thomas, Robert L. *New American Standard Hebrew-Aramaic and Greek Dictionaries: [Including] Hebrew-Aramaic and Greek Dictionaries.* Updated ed. Anaheim, CA: Foundation, 1998.

Thurman, Robert A. F., trans. *The Tibetan Book of the Dead.* New York: Quality Paperback Book Club, 1994.

Tolman, Deborah L. "Daring to Desire: Culture and the Bodies of Adolescent Girls." In *The Politics of Women's Bodies: Sexuality, Appearance, and Behavior*, edited by Rose Weitz and Samantha Kwan, 120–42. New York: Oxford University Press, 2014.

Trungpa, Chögyam, and Rinpoche. "Commentary." In *The Tibetan Book of the Dead*, translated and edited by Francesca Fremantle and Chögyam Trungpa, 1–32. New York: Shambhala Classics, 2000.

Turner, Victor W. "Betwixt and Between: The Liminal Phase in Rite de Passage." In *The Forest of Symbols: Aspects of Ndembu Ritual*, 97–110. Ithaca, NY: Cornell University Press, 1967.

Wainwright, Elaine M. *Women Healing / Healing Women: The Genderization of Healing in Early Christianity.* London: Equinox, 2006.

Weissenrieder, Annette. *Image of Illness in the Gospel of Luke: Insights of Ancient Medical Texts.* Tübingen: Mohr Siebeck, 2003.

Wills, Lawrence M. "Introduction and Annotations on Mark." In *The Jewish Annotated New Testament*, edited by Amy-Jill Levine and Marc Zvi Brettler, 55–95. New York: Oxford University Press, 2011.

Yang, Youngsoo. *Jeju's Myths in the World.* Tamra Cultural Studies Series. Seoul: Bogo, 2011.